12—

Treviso

Vicenza

Mestre

Padua

R. Adige

Venice

R. Po

N

W — E

S

Ferrara

ADRIATIC
SEA

Bologna

Imola

Ravenna

Sole

Forli

MOUNTAINS

Rimini

Pésaro

Florence

R. Arno

Urbino

Ancona

Sansepolcro

Arezzo

R. Tiber

Gúbbio

Cortona

L. Trasimeno

Perúgia

Assisi

TOWNS OF THE RENAISSANCE

Travellers in Northern Italy

David D. Hume

J.N. TOWNSEND PUBLISHING
EXETER, NEW HAMPSHIRE
1995

Printed in the United States by
BookCrafters.

Published by
J. N. Townsend Publishing
12 Greenleaf Drive
Exeter, New Hampshire 03833
603-778-9883

Type set in Monotype Bembo using
Macintosh PageMaker 5.0.

Portions of *The Italians: A Full-Length Portrait Featuring Their Manners and Morals*, by Luigi Barzini, copyright © 1977, were reprinted here with permission from Macmillan.

Hume, David D. 1928–
    Towns of the Renaissance : travellers in northern Italy /
David D. Hume.
        p. cm.
    Includes bibliograhical references and index.
    ISBN 1-880158-07-8
        1. Italy. Northern--Description and travel. 2. Renaissance-
-Italy. 3. Art, Renaissance--Italy, Northern. 4. Hume, David D.,
DG601.H86 1995
    914.5'1--dc20   95-6847
                                                 CIP

Towns of the Renaissance

Also by David D. Hume

Blueberry
A Boat of the Connecticut Shoreline

Contents

ITALY

GERMANY

SWITZERLAND   AUSTRIA

FRANCE   DOLOMITES

ALPS   •Bolzano   SLOVENIA

•Milan   Verona• Padua•   •Venice

Turin•   CROATIA

Genoa•   APENNINES   ADRIATIC SEA

•Bologna   BOSNIA-HERZEGOVINA

Pisa•   Urbino•

LIGURIAN SEA   •Florence   •Assisi

•Siena

CORSICA   Orvieto•   APENNINES

•Rome

SARDINIA   Naples•   Taranto• •Lecce

TYRRHENIAN SEA   IONIAN SEA

•Palermo   SICILY

Syracuse•

Hale

AUTHOR'S NOTE

THIS BOOK records experiences remembered from our much too short excursions in northern Italy. My wife Cathy and I learned a lot about that wonderful country while we were there and perhaps twice as much by reading about it both before and after we went on these visits. Upon such a brief acquaintance it is presumptuous to offer a book on a subject with such vast ramifications. I am not an art historian or a scholar of Renaissance history.

But each person or each couple can become experts as lovers of Italy. The country is a good teacher of its own virtues, so delightful and so compelling that the occupation of being a tourist in Italy makes every neophyte want to share his discoveries. We are apologists for the country, its language, its history and its people. This book presents no more than an introduction to a few cities where the great intellectual and artistic changes of the fifteenth and sixteenth centuries took place. If my research has been superficial and our coverage incomplete, our enjoyment of Italy is sincere. We hope our account may give other first-time travellers help at the outset or pleasure in remembering their own voyages of discovery.

My thanks to Jeremy Townsend for providing much good advice while urging me on with great patience. Most of all Cathy Hume, loveable critic and fellow traveller, always communicated a belief in the final product even when reading the smallest scraps of an uncertain design.

D.D.H.
Wilmington, NC
Salem, CT

PREFACE

THE LITTLE BROWN building didn't look very promising as we approached it after paying for tickets in the small museum shop. There was some pipe scaffolding and plastic tarpaulin drapery over one end. We entered through a low door and blinked momentarily in the lower light level.

And then we saw them. Huge panels of painted figures on the walls, huge paintings, dozens and dozens of them in reds and blues, in buff, ochre, and umber modeling. Row above row of great frescoed panels showing landscapes and cities, shepherds, donkeys, angels, Magi, Pharisees, sinners, bystanders, and penitents, covering the entire walls of the Scrovegni Chapel with a complete Last Judgment over the entrance door. The colors are so rich, the figures so human, the story of the coming of Christ, his life and death so explicit, so overwhelming, so persuasive that we realized this was why we had come to Italy, to Padua, to be enveloped in this middle-sized room that Giotto had transformed into a place of assent and of worship in the first few years after 1300. In the process he also transformed European art and started what we now recognize as the Renaissance.

Anyone whose subconscious mind was cultivated in youth by the ploughshares and swords of a liberal education must have thought about a trip to Italy at some time or other. Those furrows dug in the psyche by the experience of classical art and history are pretty much permanent. We still remember, perhaps, a few lines from *Horatius at the Bridge*, and something of the glory that was Rome when it was the center of all the world. We still wonder at the causes of the gradually accelerating disaster of its decline in the third and fourth centuries, or of the long, confused dark and savage time when the "Eternal City" shrank to become a town smaller than New Milford, Connecticut; smaller than 15,000 more or less miserable people patching up their houses from the broken pieces of the palaces and temples that once surrounded the forum. We may remember the beginnings of something more vigorous emerging from the fierce carnage of the discord among the new warlords, of bloody conflicts and mutual exilings of Guelphs and Ghibellines, of private wars and rapacious popes. Then came something better, the delight of a new poetry, a renewal of old learning, the growing civilization of the successful warriors, a rediscovery of the forms of classical design and figure modeling: the Renaissance. It seems to have dawned in the early fourteenth century and lit up southern and central Europe for the next two hundred and fifty years. In many ways it never stopped. New learning emerged from the old, and the scientific and industrial revolutions flowed naturally from its beginnings to the achievements of the inquiring and avaricious minds of the modern Europeans.

Most of these currents of thought and inventions became evident in the late fourteenth and early fifteenth centuries. Things that happened in banking, astronomy, anatomy, architecture, representational drawing, commerce, and law started in the centuries that came a thousand years after the first barbarian sack of Rome. A little less than a thousand years after Constantine moved the center of world power to the East, Giotto began painting the walls of the Scrovegni Chapel with human figures that left the chunky Romanesque and attenuated Gothic forms forever behind. In the explosion of exploration, religious reformation, artistic innovation and architectural engineering that followed, the old world of the Middle Ages was transmuted into the modern world. However held in loyalty to the church it may have been, the intellectual, artistic and architectural foundation of most of what happened in that amazing time took place in a handful of northern Italian cities, but not in Rome itself.

Italy may be politically inept, economically unstable, Mafia bedeviled, or blinded by sentiment and uncontrolled passion, it still is the birth location of much of our intellectual ancestry and we must experience it. Besides, it is beautiful, often has agreeable weather, and the food, which was deplored by eighteenth-century English travellers, is wonderful today. Those peripatetic Brits had probably been brought up on boiled beef and horseradish.

This book intends to encourage other amateur travellers like ourselves to make that first journey on their own. I write as one recently retired from regular working hours and the predictable tyrannies of clock and calendar, thus having the opportunity to take advantage of seasonal low rates at beautiful places unclogged by tourists who *must* travel in the high season. Some of us have "frequent flier" miles enough to get there and back for nothing. But even if we must pay the air fare, there is always a better deal in March or in October than in June or September.

When my wife and I undertook our first Italian trip, we were in our sixties and very much able to walk briskly for good distances. We were of an age when "sensible" shoes look appropriate by day and a woman can get by with only one other pair of footwear in her luggage. We decided to go on our own and to do without the preplanned itineraries and guided group tours offered as packages by undeniably helpful travel agencies or by the fundraising offices of our college alumni associations. We stayed at modest hotels, ate mostly in simple restaurants and moved about the country on short-haul local trains. On one trip we availed ourselves to the smallest rental car we could charter. We got a lot of Italy for our money, and we made closer contact with both city and country than tour guides could have arranged for us. In this book we hope to encourage others to do the same.

I.

HOMEWORK
Guidebooks and History Books

Do it yourself travel planning requires a certain amount of reading in advance. As in all agreeable human affairs, contemplation and anticipation add to the pleasure of consummation. We began with the current edition of Fielding's *Italy '91* and have gotten the succeeding editions almost every year since. We supplemented Fielding, which is a little weighted towards the luxury hotels, by the later addition of the budget guide put out by the Harvard Student Agencies, *Let's Go Italy 1993*, also an annually revised publication. In adding up the cost of the whole trip, guidebooks are small change. I would recommend that you try a couple of others as well. Our method was to choose the cheapest accommodations in Fielding or the most expensive from among the Harvard students' selections. We never went wrong sticking to this rule.

Sometimes the dearest of the second book turned out to be listed as the bargain of the first, as was the case in Ferrara. Then our course was clear.

The hotels and *pensione* we stayed in ranged from adequate to splendid and cost from as little as $28 per night to as much as $108, depending on the city and the extent of its popularity among tourists. We always had our own bath and usually lots of pillows, towels and blankets, although I will admit that there is a cultural difference between the American and the Italian idea of a proper bath towel.

Adding in meals, museum admissions, snacks, cocktails, guidebooks, maps and railroad fare (second class was fine) we averaged a total of $180 per day. With carefully chosen air fare we were able to finance an entire trip of three weeks and a day for just under $5000. In retrospect, it was worth twice that much.

Although the guidebooks gave us a good skeletal outline of the principal art works and how to find them, we also used the long, thin Michelin *Green Guide*. It is somewhat more inclusive of the monuments and the art works, but its comments are telegraphic and sketchy. It also provides pretty and accurate little city maps with cabalistic legends that I have almost never been able to decode. Its odd shape requires a shoulder bag with a wide side pocket to slip it in crosswise, but this made it more portable than the fat guide books mentioned earlier. The *Green Guide* does not give information on survival arrangements for food and shelter that are detailed in incomprehensible codes in the Michelin *Red Guide*. Since restaurant ratings by means of stars and forks are mean-ingless in Italy, where the simplest *trattoria* may have per-fectly wonderful food, we eliminated that one and even-tually took to garnering local recommendations from the desk clerk or the owner of the *albergo* where we were staying. You get what you pay for in most Italian restau-rants and the menu posted by law in the front window is a pretty reliable guide. I don't think we ever had anything but a good dinner on any of our trips (although a couple of the lunches were less than perfect). And we never ex-perienced a snooty waiter in Italy.

The trouble with all the guide books, and there are a great number of them, is that no single volume gave us quite enough information and each was short on the his-torical background and artistic history of what we were going to see. Our journeys were greatly enriched by do-ing quite a lot of very pleasant homework in history and art books ahead of time and between trips. If we didn't remember it all, much of it did come back to conscious-ness when we were confronted by the very stuff of Italy.

By far the best book we found was H.V. Morton's *A Traveller in Italy,* last reprinted in the 1970s and now, sadly, out of print. We found our copy in a second-hand book-store. Others may be as fortunate or able to locate it in a library. Paul Hoffman's *Cento Città* is quite good on the smaller cities and towns, but it leaves out places the size of Bologna and larger. There are more or less understand-able English-language guidebooks available at the tourist bureaus in most of the cities of the peninsula, but one must go there to buy them so they are best brought back to be perused at home. Following this method, we collected books and pamphlets wherever we went and subsequently found our second trip to Venice more rewarding than the first. But *any* trip to Venice is wonderful anyway. Much later, also in another second-hand bookstore, I found Julia Cartwright's two-volume biography of Isabella d'Este and Raphael Sabatini's *Life of Cesare Borgia*. They bring the Renaissance alive with great joy and fury.

Contributing to this spate of travel literature, I have here tried to pass on some salient stuff about a few beautiful and even some terrifying locations from the Veneto and Lombardy to Emilia-Romagna, Tuscany and Umbria, as well as a few towns farther south. We found we enjoyed smaller cities and towns more than big ones.

Reading good books about Italy ahead of time helped get us into the proper frame of mind, just as reading Mark Twain before taking a boat down the Mississippi would, or Rachel Carson before walking the beaches of the Carolinas or the rocky shores of Maine. We are able to really see only what we know well enough to recognize when it is there, right under our eyes and noses. Things we didn't know about on our first visit are, like the non-barking dog in Sherlock Holmes' *Silver Blaze,* likely to be invisible when our senses are occupied with many new impressions. There's hardly a bare brick wall in Siena that doesn't enclose some bloody tragedy or ecstatic vision, some poignant love story, mayhem or artistic gesture.

On the other hand, we found much in Italy that is

immediately apparent to anyone's eye. We used to think that the films of Fellini and the operas of Donizetti and Verdi were great feats of artistic invention. After spending even our first days in the country we realized that the former had a genius for recreating in front of the camera what goes on in all Italian markets, homes, piazzas, bedrooms and churches every day of the year. The two operatic composers merely gave a musical setting to what the Italians have felt about themselves and the meaning of love, honor and parting since they began that long climb back from the collapse of the Roman Empire.

A great number of Americans who have the time to travel think foreign lands are intimidating, especially those where not everyone speaks English. Thus many select a group tour by bus. I am sure there is fun and even companionship to be found that way, but this book is an apologia for the self-guided tour and an attempt to convince friends that we need not take our adventures in such a regimented form. The fun of cruising around Italy on impulse should not belong exclusively to the college kids with rucksacks on their backs and packs on their fannies. We think that mature adults also will, in fact, have more fun finding their own way around Italy. It is after all, a country which for centuries has been used to tourists and is well set up to receive them. Most touristic services are controlled in price by governmental decree. Government ratings of hotels and *alberghi* are reliable. In the northern cities we visited, street crime is rare and service personnel are both helpful and honest. Taxi driving is much more of a dignified vocation in Italy than the temporary pas-

time of marginal characters or scoundrels that it can sometimes be in large American cities. None ever took us for
a ride, even when we looked hopelessly confused. Several gave us excellent advice. One examined our costume and baggage and offered the opinion that we would
not stay at the bargain-priced hotel we named for more
than a one-night stand. He was right: it was the only
really grubby hotel we experienced on any trip and we
should have followed his advice. He also pointed out an
excellent little bar and café for lunch. Similarly, waiters
in restaurants were reliable fountains of information about
the towns we visited. The innate courtesy and politeness
of Italians will come as a pleasant surprise to most big
city Americans. It may well be a shock to New Yorkers.

Piazzetta Castelvecchio, Arco di Gavi   Verona

II.

THROUGH MILAN TO CREMONA
Starting in a Small City

W E TOOK Alitalia to Milan on one of our trips to Italy and will do so again. Their transatlantic planes are comfortable 747s with seats pitched to give a little extra leg room; the food is excellent, departure and arrival schedules are convenient, and the nice, bilingual cabin attendants got us accustomed to some clearly enunciated Italian before we were faced with the immediate necessity of distinguishing hot and cold from *caldo e freddo*.

When you arrive in Italy, you will need to have some money. Large American banks at home can buy you some *lire* at a not-too-terrible exchange rate. Bring $100 worth when you come and then get more on a Visa or Amex card ATM at an Italian Bank. Banco National di Lavoro and the Italian American Bank have lots of branches with cash machines that will give you 300,000 Lira at a clip. In trying to figure out how much things cost in home currency, we got used to thinking in terms of the worth of 100,000 Lira: a little more than $60 most of the time we were there. Going the other way, calculating 1,620 Lira to the dollar, required an ability to do mental multiplication beyond my skill. The public *cambio*, travellers checks, or even trading dollars at a bank window will produce a really meager rate of exchange. Visa or Amex cards are much the best deal, giving you the wholesale rate of exchange, even if they do charge you interest for a couple of weeks use of the money.

Milan is a better place to get started than Rome. If the northern city is a little more busy and commercial, there are a number of reasonable hotels in the vicinity of the Duomo. But even better, there are places like Cremona and Verona within a two-hour train or automobile trip. Once we got a car at Malpensa and drove to Como by the lovely lake to sleep off our jet lag in style at the Hotel Metropole et Suisse. But since we arrived in Italy at 9:30 in the morning, there was also plenty of time to take the bus in to the Stazione Centrale of the state railroad in Milan and get one of the frequent trains to Verona or to Cremona. Either trip takes an hour and a half and you can be settled into your hotel in time for an afternoon nap and some recovery from the disorienting shift of living in a world six hours ahead of time. If you need lunch under way, some trains have bar cars or full-sized diners. There is a large poster board on every railroad platform with symbols showing the make up of each train, including such facilities. Cars are labeled with numbers 1 or 2 to indicate class and are decorated with symbols showing whether or not you may smoke inside. Second class is just as swift, clean and civilized as the best to be found on Amtrack, even if the seats are a little less luxurious. Fares are modest and we saved money by not using the various rail passes offered to tourists. Most of these are discounts off first-class bookings. You have to do a powerful lot of long range travel to profit much from them. For short hops around the north, rail tickets are quite cheap.

All things being equal, we would recommend Cremona for a first night in Italy. In the pattern of seeking out Fielding's lowest hotel tariffs we put up at the Astoria, a pleasant little hotel in a splendidly central location and equipped with a nice little lobby bar for cocktails or breakfast. We were a minute's walk from the piazza that fronts on the cathedral, the campanile and the Palazzo Comunale. That building is a remodeled thirteenth-century palace which has a sumptuous display room upstairs that contains four of the world's most famous violins, now the property of the town, although played from time to time by visiting musicians. They are examples of the greatest of the Cremonese violin makers: two Amati, one Guarnerius, and one Stradivarius. The great stairway to the Violin Room is more easily walked down than up. It is a magnificent piece of architecture, but it is nice that there is now a lift to get to the top.

Cremona has a pleasant little park in the midst of things, featuring the tomb of Antonio Stradivari and (at some distance) a life-scale sculpture of three husky girls who may be intended to represent a modern version of the three graces. In any case they are built like true *contadine*, sturdy of breast, belly and buttocks, giving a good example of the obvious truth that the great Renaissance sculptors were not "realists" in any sense of the word. The girls who modeled ideal beauty for them couldn't have evolved to be that different in 500 years without the aid of genetic engineering. The idea of a mid-city park is unusual in Italy. This one marks the site of a Dominican monastery that was torn down in a brief fit of anticlericalism during the *Risorgimento* in the nineteenth century.

The Cremonese cathedral, known, as are all such in Italy, as il Duomo whether or not it is graced with a dome, is an extraordinary piece of Lombardy-Romanesque design that grew into the Gothic age during the three centuries it took to complete. Its campanile, il Torrazzo is a 330-foot wonder which is reputed to be the tallest in Italy with a wonderful view from the top. But a 110-meter stairway is one of the things that is really beyond the scope of such senior-age travellers as we.

The great Piazza of Cremona is a superb example of the public squares of the towns all along the Po valley. Usually they have a cathedral, a baptistry, a campanile, and a palazzo pubblico, but in detail and sense of place, each is unique to its city. In their close vicinity are the best shops and restaurants in town. By the time we had patrolled the square we were in need of the latter.

Italian restaurants open late but also close earlier than most American ones. They are used to preparing for a single sitting, usually between 8:00 and 9:00 in the evening.

A reservation makes everyone feel respected even when it isn't absolutely necessary, and is thus a good idea. At first, when we didn't think we could handle the *prenotazione* on the phone, we asked the desk clerk. He did it in style, giving notice that his *clienti* were distinguished or even illustrious people, and that he would consider it a personal favor if the restaurant would arrange to give them a good table (all of which are pretty much equal anyway).

All restaurants divide the menu into the *primi piatti* of soups and pastas followed by a *secondo piatto* of meat or fish. Vegetables and salad are added ad lib to the second half. Sometimes, sensing that the *primo* was going to be a meal in itself, one of us would order a salad instead of a meat course and share it. This sort of thing would elicit a sneer from a New York City waiter but seems expected and quite within one's rights in Italy. Antipasto or a sweet on either end of the dinner is for special occasions, but the little cup of espresso can be a *dolce* in itself. They even make a very good *caffè decaffeinato,* usually called "Haag" from the trade name.

Cover and service charges are added to the restaurant *conto* so a tip is already in the price on the bill. We learned that throwing in a thousand or fifteen hundred Lira earned us many smiling thanks and the feeling of being a big spender. *Mille grazie, Signore!* Usually we were able to get an elegant dinner for two for L50,000 to L60,000 including a half liter of a very good *vino bianco della casa.*

Breakfast in a neighborhood "Bar" or in a hotel breakfast room holds few mysteries, although the former is a lot less expensive than the latter. A *spremuta* of either orange or grapefruit is freshly squeezed, while *succo* will be canned. *Caffelatte* is served as a small jug of very black coffee alongside a much larger jug of very hot milk. We thought it the best thing we had ever had for breakfast. The crescents usually have built-in marmalade and the plain rolls and butter are often served with honey.

Although Cremona is not one of the principal centers of art in Italy, there was plenty to keep us busy sightseeing for a day and we could have spent longer. The cathedral is vast and the town is still the center of violin making of the world. The school of lutemaking can be visited, although we got there too late in the day to tour it. This is one of the few towns we hurried through, a mistake in retrospect.

In Cremona, as in all the rest of Italy, one sees a bewildering number of paintings and sculpted figures. The huge majority of them have religious subject matter. There are paintings, reliefs and statues of Mary and Jesus, Joseph and the Wise Men, Peter and Paul, Francis and Sebastian and a host of other saints and prelates that we had never heard of. To be really able to see them, to understand what is there on the canvas or on the plaster wall or ceiling, you must try hard to cultivate something of the frame of mind of the man who made the icon in the first place. Coleridge said that in approaching a poem or a drama, we must make a "willing suspension of disbelief," in order to get near enough to behold the work of art. This means that, for the most part, we must leave our rational skepticism outside when we enter the museum or church. To really see that unrealistically oversized *Bambino* suckled by his teen-aged mother who is dressed like any wealthy duchess you might come upon seated in a country cave or stable, you must, at least for the moment, decide that the Child is the Eternal One, begotten of the Father before all the ages or time or space began. Keeping that conviction in mind may be easier for traditional high church thinkers than for the more rationalistic among us. But I have been taught by intellectual atheists, schol-

Luca della Robia   c. 1460

arly Jews, old-fashioned free thinkers and contemporary agnostics who could enter into that believing, often even superstitious frame of mind while in the presence of the achievements of Italian art. Let the artist instruct you; strive to understand his language. When we see Bernini's Theresa in ecstasy, we must attempt to understand and even accept the theology of a "beatific vision" that brings that expression of sexual abandonment to her enraptured face. Seeing powerful or even cruel military men who have posed kneeling around the manger in Bethlehem, think with them about why they were on their knees. In the presence of the greatest works of art, it is sometimes easy to be carried along by the belief of the artist. Sometimes, such assent is almost forced upon us by the stunning achievement of the painter. The artist is usually more persuasive than the theologian.

III.

UNDERSTANDING ITALIAN AND ITALIANS
*Non lo parliamo abastanza bene and we make
plenty of mistakes*

SETTING OUT in an airplane for a foreign land was enough of an adventure in itself without adding the uncertainty of where we would sleep the next night. Choosing a port of entry, we looked up phone numbers, country and city codes in Fielding and worked out the approximate cost of a middle-rate hotel. I had memorized a few phrases in Italian, wrote myself some crib notes and dialed. Happily I got an English-speaking clerk. This linguistic miracle, I learned, comes with virtually any hotel that charges the equivalent of $80 or more for a double room. We were able to find better bargains later on when our Italian improved.

Between that first intercontinental phone call and the actual air trip, we had several months to prepare. Like most Americans we didn't read or speak Italian and, regrettably, had lived with the conviction that acquiring a foreign language is just too difficult a thing to attempt in the golden years. We had read in a newspaper that the Prince of Wales thinks that even people of his tender age are too old to learn another language. We set out to prove him wrong. We gave it a try and were amazed at how much progress we made. Our study included ten lessons with a tutor, a lovely young lady who later commended us to her brother in Verona. We also did a portion of a semester in a $20 course, taught by a charming bilingual Scot, at our local Senior Center. Most of all we discovered that my wife learned what she read and I learned what I heard. We both learned quite a lot with very little pain. Even though I don't memorize poetry now with the same speed I had in my teens, tapes, modern methods and a grown-up frame of mind made a huge difference from my experience in high school.

It is possible to tour Italy easily without knowing any Italian at all, but in that case we would have probably stuck to the slightly more expensive hostelries where one can count on someone being on hand to translate. I had a comic interaction with an obliging chambermaid in Florence while trying to acquire an extra pillow until we accidentally discovered that the word "cushion" worked in both languages.

I learned a lot of the basic language from the tape cassettes that proclaim boldly that you can speak Italian in a few days! Despite some exaggeration, they turned out to be wonderful for starters. Italian is easy to pronounce for English speakers and there are a lot of cognate words.

The trick turned out to be to hear the tapes again and again (they go on when you turn the key in the ignition) and, after twenty or thirty repetitions, I had the first tape memorized. I then invested in another one from a different publisher. For the basics it works.

Italian is an inflected language; that is, word ending changes convey the grammar and the use of the words. So tapes that also teach verb forms and grammar are very useful as a second step. Penton Overseas, Inc. (1-800-748-5804) puts out a series called "Learn in Your Car," which consists of three levels of two 90-minute tapes each. It starts with single words and progresses to the more exotic tenses (the conditional?), lots of useful sentences and a functional vocabulary of more than a thousand words. Penton tapes also have the nifty feature of keeping the English and Italian on the right and left ears of a car stereo. Turning the balance knob hard over lets you practice the one without hearing the other. They also give each word or phrase a second repetition with a moment's pause between so you can search your memory and repeat what is being said.

Another comprehensive set of six tapes with helpful handbook and transcript is published by Passport Books. We got them through Audio Forum (1-800-243-1234).

By far the best pocket dictionary of the many we have tried is the little green one published by Berlitz. It is small, has a durable binding, includes a good section on food and drink and even adds a couple of pages of the most useful forms of irregular verbs (a life saver in some situations). There is an Oxford Minidictionary that is very good, although a little too fat for the pocket. Middle-sized dictionaries by Cassell and others didn't seem to offer much more than the littlest ones. I finally splurged and got the Harper Collins-Sansoni dictionary. Weighing in at close to ten pounds for $35 it is a great bargain and gives all the slang, scatology, and technical words anyone would need to struggle through modern or classical Italian writing. It also gives numerous examples of usage that are invaluable for translation as well as composition. Too heavy to take along, it is the anchor of our growing library of Italian books and pamphlets.

An old war horse of a school book is *Italian Made Simple* (Doubleday). It can be pursued with or without a teacher and gave my wife (the better grammarian) a good syntactical foundation for the auricular stuff I was getting while driving the car.

The fact that learning the language was easier than we expected from our school experiences of earlier in the century probably has something to do with the social distractions of adolescence. Besides, gerontologists recommend that seniors like us should indulge in such linguistic brain exercises because they are supposed to stave off senile dementia.

Although there are local dialects spoken in Venice, Rome and pretty much everywhere else in Italy, it seems that everyone also speaks standard Italian (Tuscan) and even country folk are proud that they can do so when it is required. And, best of all, we found that Italians are wonderfully helpful and courteous when you try to speak their language. Unlike many of the French, they will slow down if you ask them to go *piu piano* or *piu lentamente, per favore.* The first successfully made reservation by telephone gives one a huge new sense of power and competence.

IV.

BOLOGNA
The Learned or the Fat

WE CAME TO this modern and very cosmopolitan city
on a fast train, speeding smoothly down the Po valley in
great comfort. We tried to imagine what travel or even
daily life itself could have been like in this same area when
the Western Empire of Rome came slowly to pieces in
the years following the Visigoth's invasion. Alaric took
Rome in 410. Britain saw the end of direct command of
the legions from Italy in the same years. The Saxons,
Angles and Jutes started coming across the Channel soon
thereafter.

In civilized Emilia-Romagna where Bologna with a
population of over 20,000 had been considered one of
the most opulent small cities of the Empire, the process
was slower but just as devastating. Records are missing
for much of the period after the mid-fifth century, but

the city was surely overrun by conquerors on their way south to the capital. A second sack of Rome itself took place when Genseric the Vandal arrived in 455 and the titular emperors fled to swamp-circled Ravenna on the Adriatic coast with what was left of their authority. There they built churches and fixed their gaze on the life of another world that was displayed in their mosaic-covered walls. If they lived in a spiritual preoccupation, eschewed conquest and the establishment of a larger order, they kept Bologna as a dependency in the immediate west where the town was in the line of battle with the Langobards who later came down to take over the northern part of the Po valley.

God knows what happened in the sixth, seventh and eighth centuries. More than a dozen generations of men and women were born, grew, fell in love, toiled, had children and died without leaving a single mark on any page we can find today. Almost none could read or write. Many faced a wretched end in war or a lingering death from infection after a sword wound from an invader, or even more slowly from famine. Some lives began in the violence of rape. We know next to nothing of these people except that most found what comfort there was in some form of Christianity. They took strength from the saints whose intercession they sought, especially from the endearing archetype, Mary, the Mother of God. If these ages were truly dark and obscure, devotion to her seems to have provided what light there was. But I know too that there were spring days and hours of real sunshine in northern Italy then as now. Surely there must have been some love and laughter for there were children born to the dwellers in Emilia-Romagna whose descendents to-day populate Bologna and its surrounding countryside. In the town and its attendant churches, priests, however badly schooled, were celebrating Mass in some form or other in the eighth century when Charlemagne stayed there on his way south to get himself crowned by the Pope in A.D. 800.

Walls around the little city were required many years earlier, perhaps in the fifth century, as soon as the central command of the Roman legions disappeared in Italy. But by the Middle Ages the general slash and grab style of political and commercial life even required defensive structures inside the town. Towers were built as part of the houses of the well-to-do; before long they were tall enough to be well beyond the range of scaling ladders. There are about forty stubs of an original several hundred towers in Bologna, and several are of enormous proportion.

By the eleventh century a pair of hostile families, the Asinelli and the Garisenda, had produced a huge pair directly in the path of the old Roman road which actually passed between them. One family was Guelph (favoring the pope's political interest) and the other Ghibelline (betting on the Holy Roman Emperor). The Asinelli tower is 318 feet in height. We don't know the original altitude of its rival because early on it began to settle on one side and developed an alarming tilt. To avoid the inevitable crash, the Garisenda was dismantled from the top down until the reduced mass stopped settling. The lower tower remains a paltry 155 feet high, set at a rakish angle. The taller of the pair tilts a bit too, but not so you would complain much about it.

DUE TORRE Bologna   C. 1120

Today the Due Torre are the symbols of Bologna, sprouting from the heart of the city, leaning more or less away from each other like a pair of slightly hostile bar-room customers contemplating a fight. You surely know you are in the capital of Emilia-Romagna when you see them above you.

Many trains and railroad stations have the same sort of universal decor and sense of place that we are used to in airplanes and airports. Popping out of the 757, through the carpeted incline of the tube and into Concourse F, we are accustomed to entering a world almost identical to the one we left a few hours before. The Stazione S.F. of Bologna is as commonplace as this. It fronts on a large plaza with a series of concrete bus islands with glass and plastic shelters where short queues of city riders wait patiently for their number to come along. You might as well be in Rhode Island.

But once you are on a city bus you can feel that you are somewhere. Talk, advertising placards, footwear, raingear, headcoverings and reading matter all are specific to the town. Milanese just don't look like Venetians while they are on their way to work. And, of course, Venice lacks buses of the sort found in Rome or Naples.

During the prosperous growth of the cities of northern Italy in the Renaissance, most, with or without an asparagus patch of residential towers on the inside, became large walled enclosures with elaborate and broad battlements surrounding them. Towns were built to withstand a year-long siege, or worse. At about the same time that modern explosive artillery shells rendered the walls less useful for defense, the other results of the Industrial Revolution began to provide support for a larger population. There came a need for new factory buildings, multiple dwellings, and the network of railroads that now connect what had been warring cities of earlier centuries. This sequence produced a pattern that still exists in many of the northern cities: a compact, walled old city *(il centro storico*) surrounded by a ring of industry which is, in turn, contained within a circle of twentieth-century suburbs. The building of the railroads in the nineteenth century allowed location of railroad stations at the perimeter of the old city, usually a fifteen minute bus ride from the duomo in the cathedral square at the center of it all. Demolition of the fortifications in some towns (such as Modena) created a park-like ring of boulevards that follow the original route of the walls. In nineteenth-century Vienna, on the other side of the Alps, the *Ringstrasse* encircles the whole medieval city and provided (besides a double tram line) such an elegant location for so many civic buildings that it gave rise to a whole style of public architecture named for that boulevard.

We got instructions for finding our hotel on the Via Montegrappa from the helpful folks at the Tourist Office in the railroad station and set forth on a bus. Every town in Italy has streets named for Mazzini, Garibaldi and Cavour, as well as piazzas remembering Victor Emmanuel or memorable dates like the 8th of August or the 20th of September. But here we traversed the Via Guglielmo Marconi (a local boy who went on to invent the radio) and then turned into the Via Ugo Bassi which turned out to be the local name for a few blocks of the Via Emilia. This is the original Roman road along which the Renaissance cities of the Po valley are strung like pearls on the bosom of the fertile plain; Rimini, Forlì, Bologna, Modena, Reggio, Parma, Piacenza, and Milano.

In Bologna it seems agreed upon that everyone should go about the city looking one's best. Shoes gleam, jackets are chic and hosiery is sheer and spectacularly in evidence at nearly full length. Bologna is a town in which it is good for an adult male tourist to wear a reasonably expensive necktie. Without one you might be taken for a German tourist or an American one. I sometimes thought we received slightly more tolerant service and more of a sense of a familiar relationship with Italians by taking on the protective coloration of respectable, upper-middle-class English. I suspect that this congeniality dates back to some good experiences with Albion in the seventeenth and eighteenth centuries or a lingering fascination with Lord Byron's extended stay in the nineteenth. This was in marked contrast to the rough handling Italy received from the French and Austrians in the same period of time. Of course the Anglo Saxon cover can be blown in an instant when ordering a gin martini with lots of ice (*molto ghiaccio)* at 5:30 or 6:00 in the afternoon.

We dismounted across from the Piazza Roosevelt and looked down the length of the straight section of the Roman road to the two great towers leaning each way where V. Ugo Bassi becomes V. Rizzoli. Both sides of the street have colonnades of either Romanesque or Gothic arches built right out to the street. Shop windows are along the interior wall of the covered space, brightly lighted and full of the best of contemporary Italian manufacture. One seldom needs an umbrella in Bologna; there are many miles of colonnades in the old city.

Our hotel, a dignified and often remodeled pile had an English name, The Palace (pronounced in the Italian fashion with three syllables), a club-like lobby bar and two elevators. It was not the best bargain we found to be acceptable in our tour, but we judged (rightly, in retrospect) that we should find comfortable landing places at the beginning and then seek economy as we got more used to the country. As far as we could tell, a government rating of even one star seems to guarantee a clean room, but a limited supply of towels and virtually nothing else. Two stars turned out to signal a perfectly good accommodation wherever we went and the advantages of a third star amounted to the presence of the color television set, slightly more space for a baggage rack, a mini fridge filled with carefully counted tiny bottles of international name brand booze and, downstairs, a somewhat snappier lounge off the lobby. We never bothered to learn of the unknown delights of four or five star hotels since, except for a bit of Italian TV, all the two extra stars promised was an alarming raise in the price of a night's accommodation. I don't think their *cornetti con marmellatta* and *cafelatte* could have been any better than those we experienced.[1]

Late in the day we found a nice *pasticceria* just off the Via Emilia. It had an upper room with low arched windows looking out on a busy crossing. After ordering a gin/tonic and a Martini made "*Mezzo mezzo con vermouth e gin inglese,*" I think we left the waiter guessing where we came from: Quebec? Copenhagen?

Outside, one flight below us, the university students crossed the corner busily, coming out from under the Gothic ogives and ancient timber overhangs of the col-

---

[1] Cities the size of Bologna, Milan and Venice are more expensive than smaller cities like Cremona, Modena or Verona. In general, rates were less than in comparable quarters found while touring the U.S. And when it comes to waterfront towns, I'll take Venice over Chicago any day.

onnade on the other side of the street. In the violet light of the late hour, a girl with the prevailing Bolognese long legs and sheer black stockings came alone across the street. She also wore a super electric azure jacket and an expectant look. As she passed beneath our window, we noted with some surprise that she was talking animatedly into the smallest cellular telephone I had ever seen. Later we got more used to it; it seems that all of the young and successful of Bologna can whip the little black folding phones out of a pocket, punch in a number, and press on through the pedestrian traffic in deep and intimate conversation. It didn't appear to be business that was being transacted. The effect was distinctly un-Venetian. Not even Milanese.

After our *apperitivo*, by 7:30, the earliest possible hour to find a ristorante or trattoria open, we came down to street level and went in search of dinner. Among the streets behind the Palace Hotel we found an unprepossessing trattoria that was already filling with guests. Our table was across from a group of four Bolognese who had a sort of university air about them. All were at least middle-aged, and they seemed to focus on an older man of professorial mien with pure white hair and a florid complexion. He also had huge white eyebrows that overhung his spectacles to the extent that when he looked down at his plate, his eyes disappeared entirely behind their snow white bushyness. When he raised his head after a spoonful of his *tortellini,* the eyes flashed out and the crinkling crows' feet emphasized his smile. The other man at the table wore an impeccable hound's tooth jacket and a L75,000 necktie. The two women were comfortably elegant. Not being able to understand their conversation was a considerable frustration and we resolved to get on with the business of learning to handle more rapidly spoken Italian.

We followed their lead and had marvelous *tortellini in brodo* followed by grilled sole and fresh spinach perfumed with a touch of garlic and olive oil. Fish is wonderful all over Italy; no one is far from the sea.

Bologna is known as *Il Grasso* or *Il Dotto* depending upon whether one is more impressed with the town's learning or its food. There are lots of bookstores, especially around the corner from the towers and down along the Via Zamboni where the university lecture halls are located. We spent a happy afternoon browsing in several and found a treasure trove of parallel translation editions of a number of standard English classics. Reading *The Rhyme of the Ancient Mariner* or T.S. Eliot's *The Waste Land* in Italian with the English original on the facing page is a great way to expand the vocabulary with useful words and memorable phrases:

> Anche il profondo imputridiva, o Cristo!
> Che dovesse accarderci tale cosa!
> Strisciavano vischiosi sulle zampe
> Corpi informi per l'acqua vischiosa.[2]

---

[2] The very deep did rot: O Christ!
  That ever this should be!
  Yea slimy things did crawl with legs
  Upon the slimy sea.

I thought for a while of using some sort of quotation from this if a waiter brought us an inferior *minestra al pesce* but I never found a situation where I thought it would be appropriate. We bought a half dozen books and had them shipped home by surface mail, a pleasant reminder of our visit which arrived a month after we got home.

The geometric, legal, civic, artistic and religious center of Bologna is the Piazza Maggiore, which is bounded by the Basilica of St. Petronius, the Palazzo Comunale, the Palazzo del Podestà, and an essential row of green grocers, butcher shops and fish markets that have been located on the north side of the square since medieval times. In the sixteenth century a very capable architect, Vignola, was hired to dignify the area by concealing the shops without cutting off access to them. He did a splendid job of it with his Palazzo Banchi, a long and narrow four-story facade composed of fifteen arches, several of which lead to open passageways into the old market warren behind. The buildings around the piazza are a wonderful example of architectural styles from the twelfth through the later sixteenth centuries. They go together without the slightest hint of disharmony. Imagine a city center today ringed with buildings by Christopher Wren, Louis Sullivan, Stanford White, and I.M. Pei, all somewhat closer to each other in time, and expecting the result to uplift the spirit and give you the sense that you really are someplace. I suppose it comes from some deep-seated sense of politeness with which architects regarded their forefathers a few centuries ago.[3]

The Basilica of St. Petronius is the oldest, biggest and most interesting of the buildings facing the square. Interestingly, it was never designed to be a cathedral and never became one in spite of being the largest church and the biggest building in town. It is about the twelfth part of a mile long inside (132 m.) and nearly two hundred feet wide. Inside the nave the arches supporting the roof are joined almost 150 feet over your head. The usual design of a Gothic cathedral was cruciform, but St. Petronius was built without transepts and thus turned out to be more or less a basilica in form. We heard that the addition of transepts would have made the church rival St. Peter's in size; and the then reigning pope took steps to prevent this by diverting money that might have gone into the building to other worthy causes.

Whether this story is true or not, the Bolognese neither really finished their principal church, nor gave up the notion that they were only part of the way through the project until well after World War II. Then, in a fit of humility and perhaps of obedience to papal desire, they declared the work complete and got the church consecrated in 1954, well over half a millennium after they had

---

[3] Philip Johnson's propped up store-front facade (of limestone!) across from the Metropolitan Museum in New York shows how the contemporary self-publicizing architect will respond if asked to do something in harmony with surrounding buildings of an earlier style. We don't have to wonder what Vignola would have done in like circumstances. It's right there on the opposite side of the Piazza Maggiore.

laid the cornerstone. The finished marble skin of the front of the building only covers the lower third of the brick-work, leaving the stark understructure standing gaunt and bare above.

But as much of the facade as was finished is truly splendid! Started in the late fourteenth century, its in-structive decoration was begun early in the *quattrocento*[4] by Jacopo della Quercia, one of the earliest of the great Renaissance masters of sculpture. Jacopo made both free-standing figures and deeply modeled bas-reliefs in framed panels around the center doorway. The creamy white marble figures suggest the full, round productions of the Greeks two millennia before his time. Like his Gothic predecessors, he tells the story of the creation and fall of man, but his figures are from another world. To under-stand the real impact his work had on this period, you should first see the naked twelfth century Adam and Eve on the facade of the Duomo of Modena. They clutch their fig leaves in attitudes of dejection, shame and terror. Jacopo's primal parents are different, careless of their beauty and their nakedness before their sin.

Even while they are being expelled from Eden, and Eve is ineffectually shielding her body with her hands, Adam almost seems to put up a fight and contend with

---

[4]Italians have a unique method of designating centuries. While formally designating the fifteenth century as il quindicesimo secolo, they speak more familiarly of the period as the quattrocento, ignoring the first thousand years of the Christian era. I suppose that when one has such an abundance of centuries to deal with as do the scholars and inhabitants of the penin-sula, it is only to be expected that they should call their familiars by nick-names.

the angel. Later still barely clothed, he digs his garden with a right good will. His wife holds a distaff well loaded with spun wool and regards her husband with an admiring expectation of his success in bringing home the bacon. The two children grasp at their mother's knees like any pair of contemporary kids begging for access to the candy rack in the supermarket checkout line.[5]

None of the Renaissance artists was a bit embarrassed about the details of nudity, either male or female. From Neptune in his fountain to the Bambino in the arms of his mother, or as an adult Christ half submerged in the limpid waters of baptism, male nakedness seems

---

[5] No reproductions of the great works of art really look like the originals. My sketches aren't intended to any more than a four-color print can resemble a Mantegna painting. They are included to help indulgent readers identify what I am writing about.

appropriate in their art. Michelangelo painted a naked Christ judging the living and the dead in the Sistine Chapel, although his loins were subsequently shrouded in a swirl of protective drapery at the command of a later pope. And, of course, there are the *putti,* thousands of them, always male and always quite mother naked, coursing about the ceilings and picture frames of the later centuries of Italian painting. Breasts are another matter; they seem relegated to the prediluvian or at least pre-Christian world, except in the case of St. Agnes who carries hers, rather gruesomely, on a plate.

Naming the great church for Petronius seemed odd to us at first. We had never heard of him before coming to Bologna and couldn't see why he rated such prominence. He is in the books as having been bishop from 431 to 450, just about the end of the civilized Roman period and the start of the dark age in Italy. His biography was composed about 700 years later and lacks the smack of first hand observation. It is maintained that he refounded the town after the Emperor Theodosius destroyed it. He is also credited with founding the university around the same time, but everybody doubts this. The beginnings of learned Bologna may be lost in the mists of time, but they are not that old. Still, by the mid-thirteenth century the city was having a party in honor of Petronius on October fourth each year and he has been considered the principal saint of Bologna since then. By 1388 the people of the free town decreed a great church in his honor, not a cathedral, but a civic and religious center. Its location on the surface of the globe is reliably defined by a white marble stripe in the pink stone floor of the basilica that traces the true north/south line of the meridian.[6]

There is lots to see in the enormous basilica, especially the pair of frescoed crucifixes by Giovanni da Modena. He also supplied a wonderful cycle on the Three Kings. Some of the reliquaries containing bits and pieces of the holy (including the head of Petronius) are curiously contrived. The high Gothic polychromed wood carving is wholly unlike della Quercia's great Renaissance doorway. But for all its distance from his or our time and place, it speaks more clearly to me than the late baroque and rococo stuff that came along a few hundred years later. The tomb of Napoleon's sister looks like something from another planet as, I guess, he and his family really were.

The church has two enormous organs which face each other across the choir. They were built about a hundred and twenty five years apart in the fifteenth and sixteenth centuries. A lot of music has been composed for the pair. We missed hearing them going with all stops out. I'd like to go back someday to hear what they can do on a feast day.

---

[6] The line was laid out by Giovanni Domenico Cassini in the middle of the seventeenth century. Cassini was one of the great observers in the early days of the telescope. He found a hatful of satellites around Saturn as well as the largest division in its ring system. He taught astronomy at the University, but when he became famous he was tempted away to the Paris observatory by the emoluments offered by Louis XIV. Later he found the polar caps of Mars, and, by timing their rotation and comparing data from America, made a pretty good estimate of the distance between the earth and the sun. Never having been a fan of the *L'etat c'est moi* school of monarchy, I rather wish he had stayed on as a faculty member at Bologna.

Outside, we passed the stolid, depressed gypsy women seated at the doorways with their cardboard signs proclaiming that they are Yugoslavian refugees. I am always hesitant about beggars. Most seem too professional for my pity. On the other hand I am a lot better off than they, and begging for the meager purchasing power of those fractional Italian coins is a very difficult way to earn a living. Even if they are good at it, they aren't getting rich.

High on the wall of the Municipal Palace, stage left of the basilica, there is a glowing terracotta Madonna holding up her perfect Child for all to acknowledge. It was done by Niccolo dell'Arca in 1478, the date displayed in large Roman numerals across the corbeled pedestal she rests on. The brilliance implied by the modeled rays on the background seem to come from the child Himself. His mother, much the larger figure, seems to be a background making him visible to us but in no way calling attention to herself. She is as lovely and as modern as any of the Bolognese girls coming through the square on their way to class. Niccolo's idea of the perfection of this "sole boast of our fallen race" speaks through time without any diminution at all. He got it right: she's as good as they come. Art, as usual, is far more persuasive than theology.

Around the corner of the agreeable bulk of the Palazzo del Podestà is a little piazza, a sort of panhandle to the Piazza Maggiore. From it you can look at that part of the Podestà called the Palace of King Enzo. Enzo wasn't king of Bologna; far from it. He was the beloved illegitimate son of the H.R. Emperor Frederick II.[7] He was also King of Sardinia. His horse was killed under him at the Battle of Fossalto in 1249 when the Modenese were vanquished by the Bolognese, and he was captured along with a lot of valuable loot, some German soldiers, and three thousand other prisoners. His father promised "enough silver to circle the walls of Bologna" to get him back unharmed, but the Bolognese kept him for the rest of his life. The royal hostage gave them greater security than any city wall could provide. He was locked up in state in the Podestà Palace in a couple of rooms that looked out on the *piazetta*, then empty save for the pigeons that perpetually feed there. Only twenty-two at the time, he understandably found the confinement trying even though he was treated and served as a king. Once, after who knows how long in the royal slammer, he saw a beautiful girl feeding the pigeons in the square below his barred window. An introduction was arranged by one of the Asinelli. (You remember the family that built the taller tower?) Her name was Lucia. When introduced to the damsel, the young king, taking what must have been considered a rather direct approach even in those days, said, *Anima mia, ben ti voglio!* (My soul, how I desire you.) Thus, when she later bore a son, the bambino was given the surname Bentivoglio. From him sprang the line of dukes that ruled Bologna for the greater part of the middle ages and the early Renaissance. After all, they were descended from a

---

[7] Frederick was considered the wonder of the world, and has gone down in the books as *Stupor Mundi*, an appellation of intriguing innuendo.

king, even if he was one who spent most of his life in captivity. Actually, I think the Bolognese were quite nice to allow him the company of a young woman of such legendary attractiveness. I hope they were pleased with the resulting rulers they acquired therefrom.

A few hundred years after the royal prisoner's romantic assignations, the Bentivoglios being fully in charge, and the Renaissance passion for classical mythology having temporarily supplanted the outdoor display of saints, angels and the Madonna, a huge statue of Neptune was commissioned to ornament the little square. It was done by a French sculptor, Jean Boulogne who, unlike Cassini, gave an Italian form to his name, Giambologna.

The father of the oceans stands relaxed, enjoying his broad-shouldered nakedness in sunshine, rain or snow. There is a mature grace to his hefty body, powerful but not muscle-bound; his weight is on his left leg, his right foot scratches the back of a gamboling pet dolphin. He surmounts a pedestal of rosy Verona marble, holds his trident lightly and gestures mysteriously with his left hand. The Bolognese call him *il Gigante*.

Beneath Neptune are a group of bronze *putti,* usually with pigeons ornamenting their curly heads. Below them a quartet of immense mermaids (or perhaps harpies) squat facing the four corners of a huge marble basin. Unlike more conventional mermaids, these have divided thighs covered with bronze scales terminating in paired fish tails. They clutch and seem to squeeze their breasts from which sprays of water provide an allegory for the mythical rivers of antiquity. The whole is decorated with

"IL GIGANTE" - BOLOGNA
1563

the armorial bearings of Pope Pius IV, considered to be an enlightened ruler of the city, and obviously a patron of catholic taste.

We visited a score of churches in Bologna. Here, as in all of Italy, they are the repositories of the great art and are museums without entrance fees. They also keep museum hours: most of them close for two to three hours after lunch, giving us another good reason to plan our itineraries in order to get back to the hotel for our own

nap (pisolino) when most of the rest of the town is shut
down anyway.

Among the best of the Bolognese churches is the
architectural melange known as the Basilica of Santo
Stefano. The earliest of this collection of seven separate
small churches is attributed to Ambrose of Milan, who
had it built in 392 to house the relics of Saints Vitale and
Agricola which he discovered in the Jewish cemetery. I
wonder what inspired him to dig there? In the middle of
the next century, St. Petronius added a small church copy-
ing the design of the Holy Sepulcher in Jerusalem. The
Langobards continued to enlarge the cluster of buildings
after they fought their way into the town in 727. Although much restored and changed over the millennia,
these are impressively ancient places of worship.
Charlemagne stopped here to hear Mass on his way to
Rome. He graciously repaid the local monks by gathering up a number of their relics and sending them home
to France.[8]

It is hard for us today to imagine the importance of

---

[8] From Charlemagne through Napoleon, French rulers of many different
centuries have practiced this method of enriching their palaces, churches
and museums. The Louvre is full of stolen Italian treasures. This record of
larceny is quite unlike the record of the English and American collectors
who, starting with Charles I and carrying on to Benjamin Altman, bought
the stuff when the Italians felt they had lots of art anyway and needed the
money more.

The French record of cultural conservation is further blotched by
their gunners who had a habit of using large works of art such as the
Sphinx in the nineteenth century and Leonardo da Vinci's clay model for
an equestrian statue of a former Duke of Milan in the sixteenth as objects
for target practice.

relics of the saints to the Christians of earlier ages. There is a legitimate economic theory that much of the trade between countries before and during the Dark Ages and the crusades took place coincidentally along with the buying and selling of bones, teeth, hair, and other body parts of holy people of prior ages. I have heard a story of a whole city being sacked in order to facilitate the recovery of the tooth of St. Matthew from a perfidious Sicilian who had provided a bogus relic as part of the town's ransom. His fraud was discovered when the false relic didn't work to restore the warrior's sick child to health.

We approached the Basilica of St. Dominic with our noses in the map. Inside this thirteenth-century building we found architecture of the eighteenth century and the extraordinary reliquary of the founder of the Order of Preachers. Dominic Guzman was a Spaniard and a university graduate. Both in his life and in the work of the order he founded he was the counterbalance to St. Francis who provided the emotional inspiration of the later Middle Ages. Dominic preached to the people, using all the resources of intellect to persuade and convert. Francis, God's troubador, rushed to embrace them.

Dominic's container is termed an Ark and it is indeed an extraordinary vessel. Most of his remains are buried about half-way up the cream, buff and pearly white, twenty-foot stack of medieval, Renaissance, and baroque marble. The front of the sarcophagus itself was done by Nicola Pisano around 1265. Down below is an altar that has a large eighteenth-century front panel with scenes from the saint's life done in the early 1530s. On the altar level are a pair of angels bearing candlesticks, one by Niccolo of Antonio and the other by Michelangelo, who was about fifteen years old when he got the commission in the 1490s. Up above there is more quattrocento work including Michelangelo's St.Proculus, which looks quite a bit like his later David with clothes on. The top of the ark is decorated with cascades of fruit and *putti* that date from the late baroque. Although at first glance the ark is reminiscent of a wedding cake, the individual sculptures and reliefs are so wonderful that they overcome the whipped-cream look of the whole.

We were guided through the side chapels and other rooms off the apse of the huge building by an elderly, very dignified guide, a sort of verger I guess, who lectured us in clear and simple Italian about what we were seeing. He took us into the retrochoir behind the main altar and showed us the amazing intarsia panels behind the choir stalls. This extensive series of wooden inlays displays a fresh and facile draftsmanship that would be hard to match with pen or pencil, but was actually done in thousands of tiny pieces of wood, cut, shaped and glued to provide a complete spectrum of shades, colors, and forms. Brother Daminiano of Bergamo, who did them, was a discovery for us; we had never heard of this six-teenth-century master who spent more than twenty years decorating these choir stalls.

Our courtly guide then unlocked the sacristy museum and showed us still other treasures, including representations of St. Dominic as fat and St. Thomas Aquinas as lean—quite the opposite of their actual figures, I believe.

I was unable to figure out the precise role of our elderly guide. As we were leaving the locked end of the building I pressed a couple thousand Lira notes into his hand. He accepted them without protest, but I then saw him deposit them in an alms box as he walked away, making me feel like the classic crude, rich American tourist who missed the point: he was working for love. His courtesy and his dignity bespoke religious conviction as well as human kindness. Some men become pious in their later years. Some become scholarly. A few become both, as did this grand old man who led us through the treasures of the basilica.

Although it is not appointed with painting and sculpture as the churches are, it seems to me that the real spiritual center of Bologna is the Archiginnasio. Although it dates only from the sixteenth century, this is the earliest surviving building that houses the university. No one really knows when the *Alma Mater Studiorum* began, and for centuries it really had no permanent buildings of its own. Sometime, probably well before the year 1000, perhaps as early as 890, students gathered in Bologna and hired scholars to lecture and teach them the remembered principles of Roman law. The university was both old and famous before the first half of the twelfth century when young Thomas à Becket came to study. So did Dante, Petrarch, and (coming from Poland) Copernicus. The entire conduct of the school was for centuries in the hands of the students who allowed the faculty only the authority to grant degrees, an arrangement that would have horrified American college administrators if it had even been suggested by the "radical" students of the 1960s. There are reputed to be something like 65,000 students currently enrolled in all the faculties, making the old Alma Mater Studiorum by far the biggest enterprise in Bologna.

The halls and loggias of the Archiginnasio are decorated with thousands of the coats of arms of young men who studied there over the years.[9] This seems a much more civilized way of leaving a memento of one's passing than carving a set of initials in the woodwork of Old South Main, but both stem from the same impulse to eternalize the "shortest, gladdest years of life." The most exciting room of all turns out to be a reconstruction: the *Teatro Anatomica*, which took a direct hit from an Allied bomb in World War II. The building was destroyed, but, amazingly enough, among the splintered remains were found a number of the wooden sculptures that adorned it, including the damaged but salvageable studies of "skinned" men, their full musculature observable to the students. All the pieces were gathered up, and from existing drawings and plans, the famous old medical school room was put back in its original form with bare pine and cedar walls detailed into elegantly classical panels and pilasters. Somehow there seems to be no touch of Williamsburg or Disney in any reconstruction in Italy. It

---

[9] There were women too, although I don't know if any left coats of arms on the soffits of the hallways. Women were also professors of the law. Shakespeare's Portia would have presented no surprise when she pretended to be a learned, if youthful, dottoressa of the law.

is, after all, the very spot where the modern study of anatomy really began, where the theoretical scholasticism of medieval medicine began to give way to scientific investigation.

When the great minds of the Renaissance started to search inward for the mysteries of the body and to look out beyond the bounds of our planet, they had to get through the boundaries set up by an unsettled and somewhat nervous medieval church, many of whose leaders saw the new learning as a powerful deterrent to obedience at the least and a deterrent to faith itself at the worst. While Rome forbade dissection of cadavers, presumably as a matter of theological certainty that all the parts would be needed for use again after the last trumpet had sounded, the Bolognese took a different course. The bodies of executed criminals were given to the university medical faculty to be dissected on a marble slab in the middle of the room while as many as several hundred medical students watched from the ranks of raised benches.

From positions on the faculties of the old universities of Pisa, Padua, Bologna, and others, astronomers like Galileo looked out upon a newly discovered universe and anatomists peered deep within the human body. Both were undeterred by the strictures of the timid orthodoxy of their time. And learning such as theirs, once out of the box, cannot be confined again.

V.

FERRARA

A City of Intelligent and Beautiful Women,
a Few of Whom Were Very Rich and Powerful

Bologna and Venice, enormously different as they are, seem at least to be occupying the same time zone of history. Both are very cosmopolitan cities. One would feel quite unsurprised to encounter a movie star or television personality on the streets of either one. Not so in Ferrara. This town has a simplicity, almost a naiveté, about it, as though it belonged to another time and hadn't yet, quite joined the later twentieth century, much less being ready for the twenty-first.

One of the best simple hotels we found in Italy was the Albergo San Paolo: recently remodeled, well-appointed, clean, and charging about $38 a night with shower and plenty of towels. Its location just inside the old city wall was beside an innocently empty square less than a five-minute walk from the Duomo. There is a cheerful little bar next door that provides jam-filled buns and cappuccino for breakfast.

The morning after our arrival, we woke to find the quiet space in front of the albergo filled with panel trucks, trailers and small-scale RVs. Poles and awnings were sprouting in various directions from the vehicles and a multitude of folding tables were being filled with merchandise. Evidently, we had hit upon the day of the weekly market. Sweaters, cheese, foundation garments, shirts, tools, bras in an amazing variety of sizes, socks, *gelato* in many flavors, Coca-Cola, rain coats, and shoes with stiletto heels were laid out in profusion at prices set to attract the common man and woman. I found a couple of pure cotton handkerchiefs printed in paisley patterns and sporty colors. Very much the thing for the breast pocket of the blue blazer I wore all over Italy.

Progressing into the centro storico, we began to hear the hesitant strains of a semi-professional military band, mostly trumpets and drums. The bandsmen, some of them boys and girls, were gathered in the courtyard of the Palazzo Comunale. They accompanied a squadron of costumed men of mixed ages who were carrying fluttering black and white checkered flags which they waved in unison and hurled into the air to catch with a flourish as they descended. Breaking into two ranks they took to tossing the flags back and forth over a widening space between their leaders. The band played while a largely nontouristic crowd admired their skill and applauded. After a while the musicians formed into a parade and led the populace down the street to the cathedral where they shaped up to salute a sizable contingent of people in mufti who filed into the church. Many wore colored ribbons in their lapels, and we eventually learned that the whole affair was a salute to the blood donors who were going to have Mass celebrated in their honor. It all seemed an expected and appropriate way to encourage civic virtue.

The very center of Ferrara is the castle of the Este family. Niccolo III built it and dug its moat (which is clear, being fed by a freshwater spring) to protect himself and his family after 1385, the year in which they had a close go with an uprising brought on by too stringent a tax policy. This is one of the few cases of a large chunk of military architecture being dedicated to protecting the ruler from his own people.

The Estense took a firm hand in most things. Niccolo later discovered his attractive young wife *in flagrante delictu* in the arms of his own bastard son. You can visit the dungeon where he briefly chained them up before having them beheaded. I have read that both Donizetti and Mascagni made operas based on this regrettable affair, but I have been unable to locate either in the Metropolitan Opera's reference book. Perhaps they are sung only in Europe. Browning's *My Last Duchess* attributes a similar style of family discipline to another duke of Ferrara who thought his wife responded too readily to the compliments of a monkish painter whom he had hired to do a likeness of her.

Ferrara in the fifteenth century was four times the size of Rome and the most brilliant court of Europe. A bit later, writers Torquato Tasso and Ludovico Ariosto lived

here and found the intellectual climate stimulating. The
real center of all Ferrara's activity was to be found in the
influence of its women. Ercole I, Duke of Ferrara, had
two daughters, Beatrice and Isabella d'Este. The girls were
not only beautiful, they were intellectual, educated, and
possessed of the taste that set the fashions for quattrocento
Italy as well as the rest of Europe. Beatrice eventually
married the Duke of Milan, Ludovico Sforza; and Isabella
married Gianfrancesco Gonzaga, the Marquis of Mantua.[1]
Their brother, Alphonso I, in a stroke of happy political
good fortune, acquired the daughter of the Pope as his
wife.

Lucrezia Borgia had two husbands before Alphonso.
One died under questionable circumstances (strangling?)
and the other was annulled out of the way on grounds
that impotence made consummation of the marriage

---

[1] Isabella was a spritely fifteen year old when she married and moved to
Mantua. She wrote home to her unmarried sister to say, "I am yoked to a
ducal stable boy who belches, farts and spits on my train as readily as he
slobbers over my hand." Yet the marriage was a long and relatively faithful
one and did honor to both. He provided financing for Giulio Romano's
lovely Palazzo del Te where his young wife and son developed one of the
prettiest little palaces in the whole country. She wrote some pretty spicy
stuff in letters to her sister, many of which have been preserved in the
archives of the family in Ferrara. More about her in Chapter X.

There are a number of books about these fascinating ladies. At the
end of the last century Julia Cartwright wrote biographies of both Beatrice
and Isabella d'Este, the latter published in London in 1902. Although the
author was a Victorian bluestocking scholar, her accounts make good reading
today and provide copious quotations from Isabella's letters in sensible
English translation.

impossible. But even though she was being used politically by her father and her brother Cesare in all of these nuptial alliances, Lucrezia was very much a person in her own right. At the top of her form at the time of her third wedding, she was twenty-one years old, rich, famous, and possessed of long flowing blond hair that drove most of Italy wild with delight. When she came from Rome to Ferrara to consummate the marriage (it had first been celebrated in a ceremony with a proxy under the paternal eyes of the pope), the event provided the most spectacular procession in a century known for such ceremonies. In his gold mine of information about the Renaissance, *A Traveller in Italy,* Morton relates that it required one hundred and fifty mules to carry her trousseau and that in the cavalcade were a hundred male and female attendants, clowns, jugglers, musicians and an appropriate number of elegantly dressed men at arms. When she got to Ferrara, a throng of soldiers, ambassadors, and noblemen came out to meet her. The learned doctors of the University carried the canopy over her head. Her husband (who had never seen her) came to claim her in ceremonial armor made of scales of beaten gold. Although affection had nothing to do with his choice of bride, he delighted in his fortune of having married her and was heartbroken when she died at the age of thirty-nine.

Most of the stories decrying Lucrezia's morals and accusing her of poisoning enemies seem to have been made up by partisans of the popes who succeeded her father and wanted to blacken the name of the Borgia family of by making up history from improbable gossip.[2] From the time she arrived as Duchess of Ferrara, there was no mention of scandal of any sort. Her husband and four children loved her and mourned her death, as did a people who held her in affectionate regard. Her name is remembered fondly in Ferrara to this day. And one does not name a restaurant after la bella duchesa with the blond hair if there is any substance to an old reputation that she poisoned the guests at the dinner table on a regular basis.

One of the wonderful buildings of Ferrara is the Palazzo Schifanoia, a little *delizia* or pleasure palace built and decorated to the taste of some of the early Estense during the quattrocento. It was designed as a place in town where a busy duke could get away from the cares of office and the dullness of government. The name means "Banish Boredom!" Appropriately enough, it is now used as the Museo Civico and houses a good collection of paintings. But the treasures of Schifanoia are really the portions of the building's original fresco decorations done by several artists under the direction of Cosimo Tura. In a room used in the intervening centuries as a storage warehouse for a tobacco merchant, painstaking removal of overplastering has uncovered the frescoes commissioned

---

[2] Rafael Sabatini's biography of Cesare Borgia is the principal source for my own pro-Lucrezia opinions, although a number of other modern writers come down on her side. Victor Hugo, looking for a good tale for a play, seems to have done the most to magnify the sixteenth-century slander. H.V. Morton is also strongly pro-Lucrezia.

by Borso d'Este[3] to celebrate the passing of the months of the year.

Originally twelve in number, these paintings are in various states of repair, but several are in fine shape. One of the best is the representation of April, filled with allegories of spring and fertility, Mars doing obeisance to Venus, young courtiers exchanging shy kisses, the three Graces showing themselves off holding hands in a corner, rabbits preening in the undergrowth.

"Schifanoia" c. 1470

---

[3] He was the illegitimate half-brother of Isabella and Beatrice's father and shared in the family's good taste in works of art.

When we had gotten to the middle of town, we found that the center of Ferrara played host to a semi-permanent book fair which was in session along the south side of the cathedral. Aluminum framed tents covered the stalls. We found reprints of engravings from Diderot's *Encyclopédie*, which illustrated all that could be known about musical instruments, as well as art books, contemporary and classical pornography, novels, and textbooks of engineering, business administration and medicine. Across the way there was a skein of inexpensive market stalls built into the exterior wall of the cathedral, giving it a nice medieval look.

Farther up the way, in the direction of the great Estense castle, the street is lined with fashionable shops. I stopped in front of a store labeled "Borsalino." Now I had heard of Borsalino, the most fashionable hatter in Europe. I lacked a hat that I enjoyed wearing, and here in the window was a pale oatmeal colored Prince Rupert style hat of alpaca tweed. So what if it was marked with a small tag quoting 90,000 Lira! I eventually reasoned that such a moment would never come again and that indiscretions committed in foreign travel are the easiest to forgive oneself in a winter of penitence later at home.

Not twenty meters farther up the street stood a statue of the original prophet of the bonfire of the vanities: Savonarola himself commemorated here as a sort of home town boy and hero where he received his M.A. from the local university, the stern young man seems to be preaching to the modern world while gesturing in the direction of the palace where the Este princesses collected art and

books and patronized poets, painters and musicians. I got
no comfort from the presence of this severe preacher who
inspired the cause of democracy in Florence at the end of
the quattrocento. His *bruciamenti della vanitá* during the
shrovetide carnivals of 1497 and 1498 consisted of ignit-
ing a great quantity of what he considered to be immoral
books and frivolous objects (hats?) in the middle of the
Piazza della Signoria. Savonarola had studied drawing in
his youth in Ferrara. He probably didn't burn a lot of
great art in the Florentine square. His ideas were inflam-
matory enough and attracted the spiritual attention of
both Sandro Botticelli and Michelangelo.

But in the short run the Florentines really preferred
the Medici magnificoes to the stern leadership of the democracy championed by the religious reformer. The Pope
(Alexander VI, Borgia, Lucrezia's father) tried to channel
his power and energy into the church's mainstream, but
the monk rejected a cardinal's hat and continued to follow only the counsel of his own fiery conscience. In the
long run his rebelliousness became entwined with political conflicts surrounding the battle between the papacy
and the French league of cities in the north and Savonarola
was ordered to stop preaching. He was offered absolution
for submission. He took to the pulpit of the cathedral
again, was subsequently imprisoned and tortured into
confessions that placed him in jeopardy of the secular
authorities. Eventually, after three trials and much popular noise in the street, he was (with two companions)
hanged in a Florentine Piazza. The bodies were burned
in a bonfire of their own and the ashes cast into the cloudy
waters of the Arno.

Savonarola was incorruptible and filled with the passion of a wholly uncompromised, puritanical Christian

SAVONAROLA
MONUMENT
FERRARA

conscience. He was powerful in rebuke of the luxurious
and simoniac popes, but he never rejected their authority
in the later manner of Martin Luther, John Calvin, or
Henry of England. He seems to have accepted his own

sacrifice as a necessary example to the church of his time. He was never considered a heretic by later churchmen. The stern visage of the statue bears a very large nose and heavy jaw. The piercing gaze accuses and is still scary today.

On our way back to the Albergo San Paolo we recrossed the central square by the duomo. A one-man band was entertaining a small crowd. Along with his bass drum, cymbals, harmonica, guitar and several other instruments, he sang most melodiously in Italian. Chatting with him after his gig was completed, we learned that he was German and also spoke excellent English. He was young and very bright, but I don't think he was making a very good living performing street music. I wonder how old the tradition of the one man band is in Italy. It would seem to go along with other kinds of street entertainment: organ grinders, street singers and the *comedia dell'arte* of the fifteenth and sixteenth centuries. Multidexterous musicians were probably coming here from across the Brenner Pass when Savonarola was a student.

Ferrara is one of the few Renaissance cities whose walls are still intact. I have no idea when they first were raised, but the parts standing today were being worked on and improved well into the quinquecento. Made of packed earth underneath, I guess, they are cased in a faded poppy red brick of a color that only old fired clays attain in time. Some groining and string courses are detailed in limestone. About fifty feet high on the outside, they are half again as broad at the top and studded with spade shaped projecting bastions at two hundred meter intervals along their nine kilometer circumference. Each of these nodes, which jutt out over a green vale or canal, is big enough to house a softball field. There is plenty of space to drive cars around the top of the wall, with walkways bordered by poplars on both sides. The whole is a mighty and impressive siegework.

Ferrara is the bicycle capital of Italy. It is set in the middle of the flat plain of the Po *(il pianura del Po)* and the pedaling is easy. The center of the city is off limits to automobiles and the whole population glides silently about on narrow-tired wheels. The effect gives the town an otherworldly quality that we found nowhere else. It is even quieter than Venice.

Walking up one of the sloping paths that communicate with the top of the wall, I met and passed a girl on a bicycle. Dressed in the characteristic short black skirt and a blue rain jacket, she steered skillfully with one hand and

held an umbrella in the other. Her face was that of a *ragazza*, between woman and child, very familiar to me. Later, I placed it. She was the very image of one of Giovanni Bellini's young Madonnas. The model might have been her grandmother by fifteen or twenty "greats." Whatever you may think of the continuation of a gene pool that would select that particular girlish countenance through that span of time, it is of note that Renaissance writers, as well as eighteenth- and twentieth-century travellers, comment on the beauty of the girls and women of Ferrara.

VI.

VENICE
La Serenissima

VENICE IS THE world's most famous tourist town. It is also the forerunner of all the theme parks that bring prosperity to the swamps and pampas of Florida and the deserts of Southern California. The great difference is that Venice used to be a very prosperous commercial city and is not populated by characters from cartoons, but by people. The city also has art and architecture that span better than a full millennium of human achievement. In the early sixteenth century Venice began to make the transition from being the active center of all that was new in the world to becoming the greatest museum of all that once had been. The change took place when the Turks severely restricted the trade routes of the eastern end of the Mediterranean and the Spanish and Portuguese followed Columbus, Vasco da Gama and Magellan to tap the riches of the oriental trade from the other way around Africa or even around the whole globe. But as Venetian mercantile trade declined, the tourist traffic started to swell and the rich and privileged of Europe began to come to see this wonder in the water. By the eighteenth century the Venetians were still building great palazzi for the rich and the trip to the city in the lagoon was becoming the *sine qua non* of a young gentleman's educative "grand tour." By the early nineteenth century it had become the most popular travel destination in Europe, a distinction that it holds pretty much to this day. The current lack of success of EuroDisney suggests that Europeans will still choose the real thing if it is available.

We approached Venice (by train) over the two-and-a-half-mile causeway from Mestre on the mainland. In theory you can arrive by air, hire a private motoscafo at the Marco Polo Airport, and come directly to the landing of your hotel by water. But that is a pricey way to get across the lagoon. There are also inexpensive A.T.V.O. buses to the Piazzale Romana and a Cooperativa San Marco boat that is middle priced and perhaps worth it because of the spectacular entry to the city. It lands you by water at the very brink of the Piazzetta, right by the Doge's Palace. From there you can get a *vaporetto* to any place you want to go. If you arrive by train you stay to the end of the line, the Santa Lucia station. Outside the grand facade we came to the *imbarcadero*, where we found the *pontile* (floating dock) of the *vaporetti* (sort of buses on the water) that took us down the canal on one of the finest introductory tours of any city in the world. Large and small palazzi line both sides of the trip and pretty soon we passed under the Rialto Bridge, the oldest of the three non-water crossings of the elegant canal. Small diesel powered work boats go by in both directions with loads of groceries, blue plastic jeroboams and carboys of spring water, baskets of laundry and the local equivalent of dumpsters full of garbage or builders refuse. Everything in Venice travels by water, and aside from the two parking lots at the Piazzale Romana and the Tronchetta; there are no cars at all. The peace and tranquility this engenders is hard to imagine in advance.

Individual tickets for the boats are modestly expensive, but we finally learned to get an unlimited ride ticket for a 72-hour period, which was a much better deal for the four or five rides a day we took. You are never more than a five-minute walk from a vaporetto stop anywhere in Venice, and bopping around town by boat is easy on the feet. No one seems to check for tickets very often on the boats, but it is very expensive if are you are caught on board without one. The fine is something like L40,000, about the price of a bottle of the best champagne, which I would rather have.

Venice is a wonderful town to get lost in, and you always find yourself sooner or later. There are little yellow signs with arrows and neat black lettering on the sides of buildings in some places, but there are gaps in such routes. Trying to get back to the Accademia Bridge or the Piazza San Marco as often as not we found ourselves at the end of an alley, dead ended at the water. Not to worry, there is always another, equally picturesque way to go.

We had previously located an attractive miniature hotel called *Agli Alboretti* a few steps from the the *Accademia* dock. We made a reservation with the charmingly accented desk clerk by telephone from the US.[1] Around one corner from the *Alboretti*, is the Gallerie dell'accademia, one of the greatest collections of painting and sculpture in the world.

Venetian painting of the medieval and Gothic periods, from the quattrocento to the latter part of the sixteenth century was focused on the eternal, things that govern the life and death of mankind: sin, forgiveness, salvation, and beatitude. The subjects were the saints, the Savior, and, best of all, the mother of God. In time, bits of landscapes and cities crept in, sometimes in stunning profusion as in Carpaccio's great cycle about the legend of Saint Ursula with all her eleven thousand virgin companions. His nine paintings fill a marvelous room in the Accademia.[2]

---

[1] My prediction proved true here, hotels of two stars sometimes have English speaking attendants at the desk; three star hotels always do. At the rate prevailing in the autumn of 1993, their charge of 160,000 Lira for bed, breakfast and tiny private bath, worked out to about $98 for the two of us. This turned out to be the most we paid for any hotel room on the trip, but Venice is an expensive city and I have spent as much or more at a depressing motel with a plastic fountain in the lobby among the concrete byways of Interstate-95 south of New Jersey.

[2] There is some debate as to the origin of the number of the young ladies who travelled with Ursula, since there is no historical record of a girls' crusade. One theory is that her feast day was recorded in the Roman *Ordo* as honoring her and eleven companions who were virgins and martyrs. The proper abbreviation for this condition is M V. Using the number, we

As the fortunes of the city began to change, it became less of a center of far flung commerce and daring
exploration. The town's talent for luxury and decoration
surpassed its expression of hope and new conquest. Painters began to include more local color and landscape with
their iconography. Even the stark apostolic subjects of
her painters began to change. Minor league saints like
Rocco[3] (for plague) became more popular than the winged
lion that symbolized the patron, Mark the Evangelist.
Eventually paintings of the city itself became popular. At
first the elegant cityscapes of Canaletto and the gorgeous
paintings of *il Buccintore,* the Doge's state barge, portrayed
the strength and prosperity of the Serenissima. But the
prosperity of the city was running down and the picturesque and curious became more important subjects. Both
Francesco and Gianantonio Guardi painted Venice not as
background but as the ultimate subject herself, and rendered her, even in decay, as being lovely in the fading
light of an autumn evening. Strings of drying laundry
began to appear in the brilliant but quickly done scenes
prepared for the eighteenth century tourist trade. Stucco

---

get a designation of "XI MV." Putting a little too thin a space between the
third and fourth characters, and a bit too much after the M, gives the
current reading of the size of the troupe. Be that as it may, I think I prefer
that marvelous army of innocents that Carpaccio saw in beatitude, being
drawn up to bliss by the Eternal Father.

[3] I should not denigrate San Rocco. In his scuola, right next door to the
Church of the Frari, Jacopo Tintoretto painted a crucifixion that must
contain nearly a hundred figures, stabbing, kneeling, nailing, weeping,
mocking, standing in for all the rest of us mankind at the horrible, inevitable, wonderful event.

spalling off the brick walls and the rotting wooden barrier doors of the water gates of palazzi along the Canal Grande became symbols of the romantic city that was quietly decaying in the lagoon off the Adriatic Sea. It is much the same today. Even though a farsighted city administration has arrested the decay at about the 1870 stage, no attempt seems to be made to clean things up to the pristine era that began to go away around 1600. If there was insufficient laundry hanging out to dry over the back canals today, I am sure a municipal clothesline office would be commissioned to recreate the romantic decline caught in Guardi's paintings: fixing the city as it had once been, forever cherished in the minds of each new generation.

One Venetian (as well as generally Italian) phenomenon that seems impervious to decay, up to date, clean, and well maintained, is the public rest room as exemplified by the one at the foot of the Accademia Bridge. It is far from the only example in Venice, and is the kind of facility that would be unthinkable in the United States. There used to be a little guidebook to the best secret Ladies Rooms in New York City. At the top of its list was the one appropriately in proximity to the ceramic objets d'art on the chinaware floor of Tiffany and Co. at 57th Street and Fifth Avenue. Just head straight for the Spode and then go around to the left to find it. Venice is far more egalitarian: any stroller crossing into Dorsoduro can come down from the handsome stone landing and find the essential rest stop underneath it, convenient to the outdoor cafe, the newspaper kiosk, and the pontile where you can catch the vaporetto to San Marco.[4]

Although Venice can be cold, even grey in the rain, its true colors are the warmth of terracotta, Venetian yellow, crimson, and gold. You see them painted as waterline boot tops on the commercial barges, in the tunics and mantles of the Magdalene or the Madonna. In the huge Franciscan church, *Santa Maria Gloriosa dei Frari,* Giovanni Bellini so clothed one of his tenderest in the sacristy. Titian gave her a crimson gown for the Assumption and painted the sky gold behind her ecstatic upward-gazing face. As the lights controlled by the L500 slot machine winked out after their counted minute, we turned back from the triptychs beside the altar and looked down the dimly lighted nave. A single shaft of sunlight from a clerestory window picked out a figure standing in the north aisle. It was a girl wearing white tights and a vermillion cape. The only contemporary in that scene, she reminded me of one of Guardi's figures giving scale and historical perspective to an early eighteenth-century painting, a genre scene of Venice.

---

[4]In his interesting book *The Italians,* Luigi Barzini comments on the wonderful spirit of such public conveniences as examples of the dignity with which Italians endow even the most humble situations: ". . . take the majestic and motherly ladies who oversee public lavatories in parks or restaurants. They graciously open doors, hand you soap and towels as if they were flowers, exchange a few courtly words, and finally accept a modest tip with a queenly nod and a smile. What better way to spend one's life, they seem to think, than amidst the shining porcelain, the roar of many waters, the perfume of such delicate soaps, in contact with such distinguished people." My wife found the same dignified attitude in the ladies room of the third circle at La Scala in Milan.

On our way back from the Frari, we came upon a
floating vegetable market aboard a pair of little barges
tied up in the Rio Barnaba. The dark green hulls of the
boats were ornamented by piles of red and yellow bell
peppers at the bow and a dozen verdant shades of lettuce,

Rio Barnaba
JJH

cabbage and spinach in wooden crates along both sides of
the cockpit. It was raining and the waterborne market
was shielded by a drooping green canvas awning strung
over it on poles. Customers stood under black umbrellas
and spoke their orders from the quayside. We had no cooking facilities or even the situation to make a salad, but the
fresh produce was so compelling that we bought a couple
of oranges and three pears for the sheer joy of participat-
ing in the fresh fruit.

Near the Rio Barnaba is the house where Richard
Wagner lived while he was composing *Tristan und Isolde*.
Somehow I have a hard time imagining him working out
the rising cadences of "die Liebestodt" on a big square,
Victorian piano in a room with a coffered, polychromed
ceiling and windows lighted by the sunlight reflected from
the lapping wavelets of the local canal, but that seems to
be how it happened. I had always assumed a ruined castle
in the Bavarian Alps with thunder and lightning playing
about the mountains. So much for my view of Teutonic
romanticism.

In good weather one can sit out in the Venetian sunshine or shade until late autumn. If the outdoor tables of
the Quadri or Florian's in the Piazza San Marco set you
up for too costly an aperitivo, there are other charming
places to be found. We favored a little clutch of tables and
umbrellas that sprouted in good weather at the south end
of the Accademia Bridge, the gateway to the sestiere of
Dorsoduro. It provided a good view of the open end of
the Canal Grande and was a fine place for people watching as the gondolas bore the tourists past. We had been
warned of the great cost of chartering a gondola, and at
first just watched the young Japanese honeymooners enjoying themselves. But later we investigated and found
that rates are regulated by the city, and a good excursion
could be had at a cost of something like $85 for an hour
exploring the canals large and small. Now that price
wouldn't have provided an hour's worth of the services of
a second-rate New York or Boston psychiatrist, and with
far less benefit to the spirit.

We signed on with Mauro, one of the younger gondoliers, and set out with him on his own route to show
us Venice from the water. Mauro explained that the right
to be a gondolier is inherited, there being a limited number of slots available (like New York City taxi medallions).
His father died early, so he came into the trade young and
was happy to support his widowed mother while he himself sought a wife. He obviously enjoyed his work and
like all gondoliers, was greatly skilled at maneuvering the
36-foot shell with his single scull. Gondolas are built with
a twist in the keel, and thus have an inherent tendency to
go to the right. Sculling with the single sweep on the
starboard side tends to send the boat toward the opposite
side. The combination of force and form contrive to keep
the vessel on a remarkably direct and steady course. Occasional steering with the dragging scull gets one around
corners, some quite sharp. Gondoliers don't sing, by and
large, but they do use a series of musical shouts and bel-
lows like an automobile horn when they approach a blind
corner.

All over Italy a ristorante is theoretically a more elaborate and expensive place than a trattoria. A *pizzeria* is simpler still, but will usually serve a number of things besides
pizza, often a full dinner with antipasto, primo and secondo
piatti from a limited selection. Wanting neither to fast nor
gormandize, we usually chose the trattorie for dinner.
One of the best of the touristic eateries turned out to be
Alla Madonna, in a sort of blind alley of the same name
just south of the Rialto Bridge on the San Paolo side. It
was less leisurely dining than some, but the food was fine

and the price moderate. On several other occasions we followed a somewhat more Venetian clientele, to the San Trovaso on the rio of that name about half-way between its ends, one canal west of the Accademia. Both of these places are popular, and we needed reservations during an October visit.

Every urban neighborhood in Italy has its bar. Not entirely what the name implies to an American, these shops serve breakfast to all Italy as well as a drink for the homeward bound in the evening. I learned that if you order your caffelatte at the counter and eat your *panini* standing up, you are charged the modest price of the government regulated schedule, but you don't have forever to keep your spot belly up to the counter. If you sit at one of the little tables your price will go up by a factor of two. But once you have taken the table, it is yours for the morning. Most bars will provide a local newspaper, but you can bring your own *International Herald Tribune* if you want to spread out and catch up on the American stock market or the news from home. I took to settling down to writing our journal and dispatching correspondence. Once you have hired that spot at the table no one will hurry you. Italian coffee is the best in the world and the ritual is a very pleasant way to begin a tourist's day. It is even said that the Italian method of sending steam through the freshly ground coffee makes a brew that is less acid and much kinder to the gastric mucosa.

There are enough museums and churches in Venice to keep one busy for months, but there are also all sorts of other things out of doors that are worth poking into as well. In the southeast portion of the great Piazza San Marco is the huge campanile that was begun in the nineth century and completed in 1513.Topped by a weather vane to give essential clues to ships leaving harbor, it stood until 1902 when it collapsed after being struck several times by lightning. It was rebuilt immediately with the modern addition of an electric lift that will bring you some hundred-plus meters to the top in seconds. On a bright morning or during one of those magic sunsets just after the storm has passed, the trip to the top is a wonderful experience.The view of the piazza below is unequaled. Even Isabella d'Este and the Duchess Elizabetta of Urbino were enchanted by it when they came to see these sights nearly 500 years ago.

Most of the north and south sides of that huge trapezoid are bounded by Jacopo Sansovino's elegant cinquecento facades that contain expensive shops and the cafés that the pre-air travel equivalent of the jet set made famous in the eighteenth century.The west end is bounded by a matching building that contains a couple of banks. It was actually built in the nineteenth century at the order of Napoleon who wanted to tidy things up a bit after he took over Venice and before he sold it to the Austrians. Much as I dislike Napoleon, I will admit that the closed end of the piazza is quite elegant.

But almost exactly a thousand years earlier than this adjustment to the borders trimming the area, the eastern end of the square saw the erection of the first version of the Basilica of Saint Mark. Dark, bulbous and brooding over the piazza it seems an almost alien presence in the midst of the Renaissance, baroque or even the gothic buildings of the town. Nevertheless, it belongs quite surely; Venice is just very old.

The Huns, Goths, Vandals, and Lombards really called this city into existence in those obscure times of the fifth, sixth and seventh centuries. The refugees who looked for safety to the isolated islands of the lagoon were at times alone, at times owned or "protected" by the Ostrogoths who ruled in Ravenna or by the emperors of the east who ruled in Byzantium. Torcello was the first island to have a cathedral: they started building Santa Maria Assunta there in A.D. 639. You can still see it today if you take the vaporetto #14 out to the island, about a half-hour trip across the lagoon to the northeast.[5] The seventh-century architecture on Torcello looks like some found in Ravenna. The weedy ruins of the island are romantic and mysterious. Once many thousands lived there, now only a few hundred.

The major action shifted to Cittanova, (the larger islands bisected by the Canal Grande) long before the end of the first millennium. By 727 Venice declared itself independent of Byzantium and elected its own duke, the first doge. Charlemagne's Franks chased a later one over to the still more distant islands of Lido for a while, but the administrative center was located at the Rialto in the beginning of the ninth century and has stayed in the vi-

---

[5] The only restaurant on the nearly deserted island of Torcello is reputed to be expensive, but the neighboring island (reached by the same boat) is the lace making center of Burano, where there are a number of nice places to eat without spending a doge's ransom for a slice of pizza.

cinity ever since. This was when they started to build San Marco.[6] There is little to be seen of this early cathedral now. Most of the present basilica dates from the eleventh and twelfth centuries. Its lead-covered domes look more eastern than western, but they don't seem totally Greek to me. After many hundred years of building and revision the church is *sui generis,* a type that if you find imitated anywhere else on earth only reminds you of itself.

Grecian Horse, San Marco
c . 300 Bc (?)

---

[6] The patron saint of the city was originally St. Theodore. Because he was a Greek, his devotion supported the implication that Venice was a dependency of Byzantium. The prosperous families and bishops of Venice were aware of the unifying principle of having one's own local patron as well as the prestige that came from claiming an apostle as the local hero. An evangelist would be even better. Learning that St. Mark's martyred remains were in Alexandria where, the city being firmly Moslem, nobody much wanted them anyway. So an expedition was organized and some sailors returned to the Doge's palace bearing the holy relics of the author of the earliest gospel, symbolized by the winged lion of the apocalypse and forever after the protector of the city.

Over the front portal are the four Byzantine horses brought back from the sack of Constantinople in 1204. Those out front are reproductions fit to stand the weather and modern pollution. The originals are in a gallery upstairs off the northwest balcony of the basilica and are very worth going to see. No one is quite sure when they were made or who did them, but they are old enough to make their metalworking an amazing feat. They are also quite beautiful, fierce, proud and in every way worthy of their reputation. Napoleon stole them away to Paris, but the Venetians eventually got them back again. The people of Venice have rejoiced in their prideful presence for three quarters of a millennium.

San Marco is large, complex and rich enough to merit several visits at different times of day. Don't by any means miss the fourteenth-century mosaics that Doge Dondola commissioned in the baptistery where a spectacular Salome dances in a high-necked, scarlet, fur-trimmed dress which complements her figure. She holds the head of the Baptist on its platter above her, dancing with a sensual animation that shows through the stone tesserae so clearly you can almost see her undulate to the music.

Later, when we had gone back to Dorsoduro again, across the Canal Grande, towards the Giudecca end of the Rio di San Trovaso, we came upon a small boatyard where gondolas are hauled to have their bottoms painted and other maintenance performed. I pushed in the unlabeled door on the land side and found myself in a dimly lit shed where there was a jig for assembling a gondola, with the keel and garboards of a partly completed boat clamped in place.

The Venetians don't steam green oak to make it bendable as we would in a wooden boatyard in this country; instead they seem to heat seasoned wood with a large propane torch and then force the sometimes slightly charred planks onto the form. It is a mercy the whole place doesn't go up in smoke during the process. I got into conversation with a boatwright in an open-doored shop on the eastern stretch of the Zattere. He was building a small motoscafo on the ground floor. When I showed him a wallet-sized snapshot of a boat I had built in Connecticut, he welcomed me in and took me up to the

Boatyard on Rio Trovaso

lofting floor above, where he was laying down another boat.

Gondolas evidently last twenty-five to thirty years. None of the wood is reused, I was told, not even the sculptured foredeck panels. Other than the black paint, no modern preservatives are used. Being familiar with epoxy/wood construction, this seemed curiously wasteful to me until I thought more about the Venetian attitude towards decay: it is a part of life in this city. And some wood lasts quite well by itself. The greater part of the city stands on wooden pilings sunk into the mud of the lagoon. They have been there for various lengths of time up to nearly a thousand years. Rot spores, molds and wood-chewing worms and mollusks cannot live in the anaerobic environment of the mud. There are said to be a million pilings under the church of the Saluté, holding up that huge mass of domed stonework. As far as I can tell, none has ever been replaced or even could be. This situation is not unique to Venice. In New York the huge granite towers of the Brooklyn Bridge rest not on bed rock, but on fifteen or twenty feet of yellow pine beams which originally were the roof of the caisson that was worked down through the mud by the first "sand hogs" who did that excavation.

But the boats do decay and decay seems very Venetian. Fresco painting, brushing the pigment into the wet plaster, is a very permanent art form in the rest of Italy, but in Venice the humidity has caused the destruction of almost all the frescoes and, aside from mosaics, oil painting on canvas is the most reasonable shot at immortality. I

noticed that the inch and a half docking lines used on the
Vaporetti to snub them up short against the landing stages
were of new blond Manila hemp, a kind of rope that an
American yachtsman would consider too impermanent
and rot prone to be considered for his boat. They check
the boats with a confusing sort of double hitch over a pair
of smooth iron bitts on the rail. Is the Manila able to grip
the worn metal better than nylon? Is it cheaper even if
soon abraided? Or is it an old Venetian attitude that since
all things decay sooner or later, one will always have to
replace ropes and lines every year or so anyway.

Walking home through Dorsoduro late at night we
came through a narrow alley and discovered a photographer with a big square view camera on a tripod studying
a little *Madonnina* in a niche with a small red electric vigil
light. There was a 60 watt bulb in a little iron basket above
the statue. She was protected by a chicken-wire screen
and the stucco around her was streaked with rust. The
photographer turned out to be an Englishman who was
doing a book of pictures of Venice, all taken in available
light. He was obviously going to need a very long exposure to record the eighteen-inch-high rendering of Our
Lady and Child. She looked as though she cared more
about the people of Venice than they merited for the care
they took of her. I guess that is the way it has always
been.

We visited the site of another Venitian lady, Peggy
Guggenheim, whose house is now a gallery of abstract
art. Having lived for many years next door to the Solomon
Guggenheim Museum in New York, I felt I was sort of a

relative.[7] But the paintings exhibited there belonged in a Madison Avenue gallery or SoHo. Abstract Expressionism in Venice only reveals how lousy most contemporary painting is when seen along side the great Venitian painters.

There are many things to see in Venice and many other things that are there or have been there that cannot be seen. One of these great creations of human art, enterprise and energy was the Aldine Press, whose mark was an anchor entwined with a dolphin. The founder, Aldo Manuzio, was a disciple of Giovanni Pico Della Mirandola, the scholar who set out to reconcile classical humanistic learning with Christian faith. Both of these men were among the futurists of their era. Aldo came to Venice in 1490, a few decades after the first printed books began circulating in Europe. He set up a printing press, and began at once to set in beautiful, legible type the Greek and Roman classics and to print them in editions

---

[7] While that museum was under construction in the 1950s, I haunted the site. Once, while watching the "great man" sketching on a stack of plans that had been piled on a temporary drawing board, he caught my eye and said "Young man, pass me that scale." I picked up the little triangular ruler and reached across the temporary table to give it to him. Ever since I have maintained that I helped Frank Lloyd Wright design the Guggenheim Museum.

I'm sorry the city fathers didn't let him do a palazzo on the Grand Canal. He could have gotten away with it, and the sense of continuous architectural history would have been grand. I guess they turned him down because the new building might have opened the way for an invasion by Gropius, Johnson, Van der Rohe and the rest of the practitioners of the "International Style" that would have been dreadful for Venice.

both accurate and sumptuous. He also brought out the near contemporary works of Petrarch, Dante, and Boccaccio. His engraver, Francesco of Bologna, invented italic type. Aldo's work became the model for scholarly publication during the succeeding centuries, and the type faces he used are still the standards by which modern publishing proceeds. This book is set in a face used by the Aldine Press: Bembo, whch was named for the humanist scholar Pietro Cardinal Bembo, a close friend of Isabella d'Este. The type face was created in the 1490s. The computer program which composed this page is called Aldus Pagemaker.

The Aldine Press flourished under the direction of the family for more than a century, printing 908 different works in all. Some were done at the rather imperious command of Isabella d'Este after she left Ferrara to become the Marchesa of Mantova. Perhaps the most influential of his works was the five volume set of Aristotle in Greek brought out in 1498, the same year Vasco da Gama got to India and started shipping spices back to Europe. The coincidence of the voyage and the book gives a shorthand version of what the Renaissance was all about.

Examining the beauty of such books, it is amazing to think of the speed with which the resulting enlargement of human knowledge was accomplished, each letter set one at a time, each form broken down after the sheets of the edition were pulled from the press so that the type could be reused for subsequent pages.

I could find no site in Venice marked as the location of the Aldine Press. But faked Aldine editions and good facsimiles are still available in some of the bookstores west of the *Piazza San Marco* where they sell souvenirs to tourists. Look for the dolphin tangled in the anchor. Some of the facsimiles are quite beautiful. Unfortunately, the real thing is today much too expensive even for museums.[8] Wandering among these shops we came upon one that sold old prints, some perhaps regrettably taken from the cannibalized remains of old illustrated books. Among them we discovered, newly matted, an eighteenth-century view of what was clearly labeled by the engraver SAINT MARK'S PLACE. It was clean save for a touch of foxing near one edge and showed the Piazza San Marco exactly as we had just seen it, awnings hung out on the afternoon side and crowded with tourists. Only the ladies were draped in longer skirts and the men gathering in conversational groups wore knee breeches and broad brimmed hats with cloaks swung back over their shoulders. There was no identification, but from the costuming I would date the engraving from the 1750s or thereabouts. The little picture, measuring about four by six inches, was charming. The proprietor wanted the equivalent of about $75 for it, (about the charge for a night's bed and breakfast in Cremona). He seemed disinclined to bargain. The shop was quite obviously a very respectable one, full of beautiful and much more expensive prints.

---

[8] Books printed before 1501 are known as Incunabula. There are a surprising number of them, all known and neatly catalogued by bibliographers such as the late Donald Wing of Yale University. The books are immensely valuable but not much read these days.

We debated and finally distilled the general principle that, when one is gathering souvenirs on an Italian expedition, it is wise to buy a few good mementos rather than something commonplace at the duty free shop. Besides, the print added nothing to the weight of our bags and wouldn't break in transit. Today it hangs in our Connecticut library and has given back pleasures of recollection far beyond its cost.

San Marco and
The Campanile

On our last night in Venice we walked down to the
Zattere and looked out across the Giudecca Canal. A fail-
ing orange light in the sky made dark blue silhouettes of
the work boats and vaporetti plying their way across the
water. The elegant shape of Palladio's San Giorgio
Maggiore marked the direction out to the entrance of
the lagoon to the east. While we watched, an enormous
cruise ship, seven or eight stories high and six or seven
hundred feet long came from the basin on our right and
proceeded slowly across our line of sight. The ship was
brilliantly lighted and looked ponderously comfortable.
The passengers had spent several days in Venice. We wondered which of the great sights they had actually seen. We
knew they had surely missed being in either Bologna or
Ferrara while on their trip and, since the ship could not
climb mountains, they would not get to Urbino either.

VII.

VICENZA
*Palladian Villas and Barns,
and a Ristorante Across the Tracks*

We came to Vicenza by car and thus chose the Hotel Continental, outside the centro storico. Equipped with a car park and convenient to the soccer stadium, which was not in use just then, it was quite within our price bracket. The lobby and restaurant were up to "commercial" standards. We were a little nonplussed, however, when we opened the shutters of our room and looked down on a lightweight motorcycle brightly burning on the side street below. It didn't seem to attract any attention, but burned for about fifteen minutes without creating the expected gas tank explosion. We took a nap and by the time we woke up a half-hour later the remains had been removed.

The following morning we walked into town and sought out the works of Andrea Palladio, the local boy who became the most influential architect since the designer of the Parthenon. Born in 1508 with the surname di Pietro, he was renamed for Pallas Athene, the Greek goddess of wisdom, surely an appropriate designation for such an exemplar of the late Renaissance. Many of his clients were the successful *condottiere* who survived the dangerous job of working for Venice and other neighboring towns by commanding their armies. Like Generals Washington and Eisenhower, a number of these professional soldiers dreamed of settling down as gentleman farmers after the last battle was won. They had money, often lots of it, but usually no title of nobility. Yet they wanted to look important in their country seats.

Palladio was their man. He designed farmhouses of a generous, but not huge scale. His designs were classical, perfectly balanced, and equipped with adjoining barns and stables to encompass the animals, the garner, and the hired hands necessary to a country home. One look at a Palladian house and you know that the owner was a person of importance, taste and substance. In the late nineteenth century, Stanford White provided the same sort of evidence of social arrival for the new American industrial barons. There are a clutch of their houses in Newport, Rhode Island, where the architect provided instant background for the newly moneyed of a later era. And, of course, White had studied the work of Palladio.

Palladio published a four-volume set of designs *(I Quatro Libri dell'Archetectura)*. The books were studied throughout Europe and America during the next two centuries. Famous country estates on both sides of the

Atlantic, in France, Germany and in the remains of Czarist Russia still bear the mark of the great designer's hand. In the center of Vicenza is Palladio's first big commission, the Basilica. It is not a church but a classical shell erected around the original gothic town hall, which the city fathers felt needed hiding in the new age. This structure required a series of openings that would let light into the arched embrasures of the older building. Palladio managed to align the irregular spacing of the old windows with those in the new facade by the use of triple openings, the central arches with columns on either side that have come to be called "Palladian windows." Today they are made by the thousands by modern window companies, Peachtree, Anderson and Marvin, to be set oddly in the gable ends of garages and over the front doors of houses all over suburban America.

But Palladio's masterpiece in Vicenza is the Teatro Olimpico, a marvelous theater that looks small but is said to seat twelve hundred. I didn't count the spaces on the curving benches but it looked smaller than that to me. The theater is quite serene and is graced by a classical fixed background scene designed by Palladio's pupil Vincenzo Scamozzi. It was used for an opening night performance of Sophocles' *Oedipus Rex* in 1585. The backdrop is a set of classical buildings built in perspective so that the audience looks up several streets that recede into a distant horizon of ever-smaller buildings. To complete the illusion of great distance, the stage slants uphill, away from the audience. When plays were given against this remarkable set in the sixteenth and seventeenth centu-

ries, a cast of supernumerary dwarfs strolled in lavish costume through the upper streets of the depicted town,
appearing because of their size to be at a great distance
behind the proscenium. Once again, as in the case of the
books of the Aldine Press, the masterful achievement of
this earliest example of a new art form proved almost
impossible to surpass in subsequent years. The Teatro
Olimpico was the first roofed, indoor theater in the world.

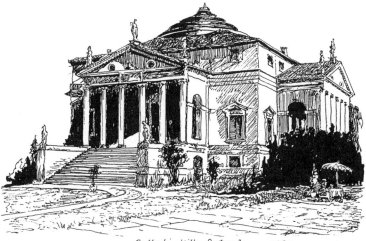

Palladio · Villa Rotonda   1550

But the real masterpieces are a few minutes outside
of town. The Villa Rotonda is the origin of Jefferson's
Monticello, not to mention half the state capitals and
courthouses in the United States. It is a nearly perfect
building and we felt it worth the voyage just to walk around
it. One of the wonderful things we discovered is that below the right flank of the formal entrance driveway is a
row of arches that lead to the stables. These openings once

gave passage to carts full of hay as well as herds of cattle on their way home and manure wagons on their way back out to the fields.

Across the way is Muttoni's harmonizing Villa Valamarana, nicknamed *ai Nani*, The Dwarfs. Besides appearing in the theater as perspective lords and ladies, dwarfs seem to have been everywhere in Renaissance Europe. The Gonzagas of Mantua built doll houses for them to live in inside their own palaces and the royal family of Spain kept them in the household where one appears in Velasquez' great painting *Las Meniñas*. At Valamarana, their statues top the pillars at the entrance, an effect grotesque but somehow charming.

Ai Nani has the added attraction of the two Tiepolos, Giovanni Battista and Giandomenico, father and son as the fresco artists of the mansion and guest house respectively. The painted walls of both are delightful and made us feel like spoiled eighteenth-century aristocrats by the time we had finished touring the building and looked out again on the serene valley below. On the other hand, caretakers live in the guest house and a homey clothesline of laundry flapped in the breeze off the perfect sixteenth-century portico.

Laundry hangs outside to dry throughout Italy, in neighborhoods both rich and poor. Italians seem reluctant to use electric dryers even when they could afford them. Electricity is almost as expensive as gasoline and they see no need to waste it on something sun and air will do for *niente*. As a result, getting washing done by the expensive twenty-four-hour laundry service that three-star hotels offer always seemed to produce shirts that were well ironed but a trifle damp when they were returned with the bill.

Feeling a little like properly entitled nobility after a day touring the wonderful villas, we were not amused to discover that the entire hotel dining room had been interdicted by the reservation of a group tour. They had arrived in their transalpine juggernaut while we were out indulging in the pleasures and amusements of their betters. The desk clerk recommended a restaurant a few blocks away and we set out in the dark to find it. After some exploration, we located the place and discovered it to be *chiuso*.[1]

At this point we met another couple walking the street in the dark. They spoke a little English and we were able to get across the idea that we were in piteous need of something to eat. They pointed us off into the night with instructions to turn left after we crossed the railroad tracks. We pressed on with great faith, through a rather desperate part of town and were eventually rewarded by the sight of a little building with red-curtained windows that bore the rather pretentious title for so small a place of Ristorante Il Tinello. Being at the beginning of our study of Italian, we were unable to do much with either the

---

[1] We got used to this word, and found it prominently displayed on almost every building in Italy between 1:00 and 3:00 P.M. When all the town is chiude, it is time to go back to the hotel and take a nap, read the guidebook or perhaps tend to each other's affectional needs as does the rest of Italy through the mid-afternoon.

menu or the voluble staccato of the proprietor, who was finishing up service to the twelve persons of an anniversary party who were the only other patrons that late at night. I finally lurched out enough bad Italian to say that we were *in i sui manni,* or something to that effect, hoping to mean that he would have do the ordering for us. He beamed, disappeared into the kitchen, and came back with a lovely bottle of Soave followed by a succession of antipasti, primi piatti, and eventually a great variety of specialties that made up one of the most wonderful dinners we have ever eaten. I have only a shaky idea of how to find Il Tinello again other than through the matchbook I saved: Corso Padova 181; Tel. 0444/500325. If you are able to find the place and eat there, I hope you will tell the *proprietario* that you came at the behest of a lost American couple whom he treated with exemplary kindness and great culinary skill one night. Also say that we will be back again and let him select the dinner again.

We saw a number of fascinating and elegant buildings in and around Vicenza. One humble structure sticks in my mind and was possibly not drawn by either Scamozzi or Palladio. Turning the car around in the dead-end of a muddy barnyard in the valley across from the Palladian Abbey of Monte Berico, we noticed a trio of large doorways. They led to a shed of indeterminate age that contained bales of hay, a wagon with modern automobile-style wheels, and a substantial pile of rusted junk. It was the sort of detritus-filled outbuilding I have seen on an old farm near Colchester, Connecticut, except that here the lintels of the doorways were supported not by rough-hewn chestnut beams, but by graceful Roman arches and slender Doric columns done in stucco over brick, Andrea Palladio's preferred materials for domestic architecture.

VIII.

VERONA
A Pink and Rosy City of the North

As MUCH AS any other town in Italy, Verona is compre-
hended by the senses: it is palpable, luscious, redolent.
This city of 275,000 has its own flavor, feeling, color, and
smell. Snuggled into the double curve of the Adige (the
second largest river in Italy), it is in October both sunny
and damp, pink and rose colored, cool, fresh with the
breath of the nearby mountains and often piquant with
the smells of olive oil and baking bread, the bouquet of
its grapes and the pungency of its geraniums.

I wonder what Shakespeare must have actually heard
about this long-lived little city on the southern edge of
the great lakes that border the Alps. He certainly never
visited it, but it merits mention or is the center of action

in three of his plays.[1] How many Anglo Saxons of later ages have used the extraordinary comparison that "Verona's summer hath not such a flower" for some perfect maiden they have breathlessly encountered. And, of course, some, by one authority or another have been "from Verona banished, for practicing to steal away a lady."

The sixteenth-century English imagined Verona as the rearing ground of the most beautiful, loveable and faithful young women they could ever imagine. Youth and social position only delay love a little where "younger than you, here in Verona, ladies of esteem, are made already mothers." And since Shakespeare so created Juliet, people all over Italy have enshrined the ideal teenaged girl created by an English playwright in their conscious and subconscious minds, mostly without having read a word of his masterpiece of hopeless youthful love. Out on the road to Vicenza are a pair of ruined hilltop strongholds named as the castles of Romeo and Juliet. In town there are houses shown to tourists as surely being the Montague and Capulet homes of the star-crossed lovers. I guess it is a little like looking at the Church of the Holy Sepulcher in Jerusalem and quibbling about whether or not it is the real thing or merely the focus of more than a thousand years of belief. When we saw the little court-

---

[1] *Two Gentlemen of Verona, The Taming of the Shrew*, and *Romeo and Juliet*. Even Othello mentions a ship "put in, a Veronese," presumably having gotten to Venice by canals that connected the Adige with the Adriatic even that long ago. Their courses are still traced on modern maps.

yard of Juliet's house, we were moved to believe.

But just at the moment we were surveying it, a bus stopped outside and disgorged twenty or thirty tourists who crowded in upon us and began to examine the statue of the girl in the cortile. It is a delicate but almost severe statue, very much late twentieth century in style of sculpture, and the maiden is modestly robed. But the stocky and bespectacled female tour guide challenged one of the men to pose with her. He grinned broadly and stood beside the statue putting his arm around the icon of the teen-aged heroine. The effect was obscene. The small left breast of the statue was polished like brass from the crude caress of thousands of such hands. One after another all the men of the group came up to take their turns clutching the brazen breast of the defenseless maiden while having their photograph taken to record their visit to Verona. It was a sort of Tailhook grab at mythological innocence, committed with much laughter and comments which, however unintelligible to us, being in German, seemed indecent. We turned away and left the conquest of that quarter of Verona to the barbarians from beyond the Rhine.

But most of the evening crowds of Verona were Veronese out for their passeggiata up the narrow but central Via Mazzini and into the Piazza delle Erbe. The streets in the centro at five o'clock are so crowded that we had to dodge from side to side to get into a stream of traffic going in the right direction. We had arranged to meet the brother of an American friend in the Café Filippina just off the north side of the Erbe, and we were glad to duck in out of the crowd. When we emerged an hour later, they were all gone.

Saint Filippina was standing on her eroded pedestal in the middle of the market square; or is she the Madonna? She seems to be serenely contemplating the canvas umbrellas and tin-roofed stalls that make the market a permanent fixture of the city center. I don't know how the places in the square are allocated, but, since they are crowded in quite tightly, I have a hunch they must be inherited in some mixture of primogeniture and squatter's rights that goes back to the Middle Ages. The size of each booth is standardized and there are no empty places, so I guess it is again, like the taxi medallions, a matter of whose family has been doing business the longest.

R. Adige at VERONA

We had a gin and tonic and a *"martini con un po di gin inglese."* Both were garnished with lavish curls of lemon peel and served in tall pilsner glasses tastefully etched with the words "GatorAide." They were perfectly delicious. The smartly dressed young people arrived in droves at five during the passegigata to meet with equally attractive and well dressed friends for tea or vermouth in a very dressed up ambiance. The café was no bar in either the Italian or American sense, and it was certainly not the working man's tavern or pub. It would have done well in a location across from the Carlyle in the East 70's on Madison Avenue in New York.

In Verona we stayed in one of the few single star inns of our trip, the Locanda Catullo. This L55,000 inn (Motel 6 can cost as much in some parts of the U.S.) turned out to be located on a pleasant little alley just off the Via Mazzini behind an almost unmarked doorway. Originally a men's club, the building was designed with some pretension to grandeur. Today there are a piano studio and a couple of boutiques on the first two floors. To reach the *Locanda* you have to climb two substantial flights (which probably explains the modest government rating as well as very low tariff).

But once having reached the secondo piano (as in all European buildings, the ground floor doesn't count), we emerged in a sort of piano nobile, a high-ceilinged loggia with paintings and mirrors as well as a rather tiny hotel desk attended most of the time by the very obliging proprietor. He provided us with a nice room with a fine shower and more than the minimum ration of towels as well as the extra *cuscino* that my aging neck requires. As obscure as his location was, he told us many people sought him out because of the plug in *Let's Go Italy*, and that the young people who came from that source were the nicest clienti he could ask for. He shared this information in a conspiratorial sort of way that implied his acknowledgment of our senior-citizen status as well as his happy toleration of the young at his nice walk-up locanda.

To make this reservation, we had been required to post a telegraphed deposit from Ferrara because it was a busy holiday weekend. At the time we stayed there the owner took no plastic and we had to wire the money order. This transaction at a post office back in Ferrara was an education in itself. Because we were checking out of our hotel, we had no "permanent address" in Italy, and although the clerk had a rack of thirty or forty rubber stamps before her she couldn't find one that encompassed this anomaly. She finally used about a dozen of them on five or six forms, clucking her tongue the entire time at the irregularity of it all. The money got there.

The day after our rainy entry into Verona we sought out our neighborhood bar for breakfast and then climbed the levee on the bank of the Adige to walk its inner curve to the Castelvecchio and the church of San Zeno Maggiore. The little city was newly washed clean by the rain, and, as in all Italian towns, the streets had been hand swept of the previous day's litter. Even the planting beds around the bushes and trees appeared to have been newly raked.

The color of Verona is unique. Besides the salmon

brick and orange terra-cotta it shares with the rest of the country, Verona has pink marble sidewalks. This lovely stone is local, relatively cheap a few centuries ago and durable. But among all these reds, oranges and browns, one comes occasionally on the ashen grey and white of Roman stonework, more of it here than in any town of such size in northern Italy. Or maybe it just seems that way because of the contrast made by the cool grey of the travertine limestone with the warm clays of the manufactured building materials.

In the very center of Verona is the greatest part of a very well preserved Roman amphitheater. The *gradini* for seating are still intact, the full circumference of the oval is complete and all the lower tiers of seats are ready to be occupied. The pale grey stone sets it apart from the buildings surrounding the Piazza Bra even more than the difference in scale and architecture. An uppermost tier of seats was once supported by a ring of eighty triple arcades that encircled the existing structure until all but four of the spans were shattered by successive earthquakes in 1117 and 1183. This fragile remnant of the outer shell is a reminder of how grand the original stadium must have been. Today it is the scene of a summer opera festival. Even reduced, it accommodates twenty thousand people in thrall to Verdi and Puccini on summer evenings. I guess this is a good reason to visit in July, since you can almost surely get a ticket. Unfortunately, we were there in October.

Verona's ruling family in the late Middle Ages was named Scaligeri, and the tribe's first real strong man was known as *Canegrande*, quite literally "Big Dog," a moniker that reminds me of a desperado in an American Western. Being known in his day as a firm ruler from his ability and willingness to discipline a subject by bashing his head in with a stone mace swung from the back of a horse. Canegrande is present today as an immensely powerful equestrian statue perched on an unlikely concrete buttress that helps hold together the reconstruction of the Castelvecchio that has been undertaken since a bomb blew away a considerable portion of it in the closing months of World War II. The raw poured concrete harmonizes nicely with the rough stone and brick of the old fortress and the brutal strength of it all goes appropriately with the presence of the tough Lord of Verona of the years between 1311 and 1329.

The art collected in the Castelvecchio is very much worth a leisurely visit and includes a lovely Nativity by Girolamo Dai Libri and a wonderful nursing Madonna (Madonna Allattante) by Tintoretto. Mantegna and various Bellini's are well represented. But one of the most surprising paintings (in Room xii) is an amazing St. Jerome in the desert by Jacopo Bellini. Father and uncle of the creators of the lovely childish virgins who cradle their breathtaking bambini, the senior Bellini gives us a wonderful craggy, desert-surrounded old man in ecstatic adoration before a crucifix with the open Bible he is translating on the ground before him. Putting holy writ into the common speech was obviously no mere work of scholarship, but of inspiration as well.[2]

We left the castle and continued along the river bank towards the great church of San Zeno. The high clouds had cleared and looking to the north, in the direction of the Valpolicella (where the wine comes from), we could see the clean shine of new snow on the sunny mountain flanks and higher elevations. A few thousand feet are the equivalent of a month's advance of the shortening season.

Saint Zeno's church is a huge Romanesque basilica that has been rebuilt several times. An incursion of Hungarians ruined it in the year 900, and it reached its present state only in the late Middle Ages. All of the lower story is round arched, but the closing of the apse is Gothic. Doorway sculptures of the original sin and the betrayal of Judas are powerful even if Eve's feet seem absurdly large. These twelfth-century sculptures contrast with Jacopo della Quercia's later work in Bologna.

But, once inside, the Renaissance burst upon us as it did on the people of Verona when Mantegna came from

---

[2] Jerome was a great scholar who lived at the end of the hegemony of Rome. He was able to travel to the Holy Land and to Rome itself when both were part of the divided but intact Empire. He singlehandedly translated the Bible from the Hebrew and Greek manuscripts available to him. But on a more personal level he seems to have been a dreadful fellow. He couldn't get along with anyone, hated company, and thought women were the primal source of sin and damnation. He lived long enough to witness Alaric's sack of Rome and the beginning of the collapse of order that followed the disaster. Jerome attributed the continuing distress of the latter age to the judgment of God on the manifold sins of his contemporaries, mostly from consorting with women. His point of view lingers on in Rome.

*Il pecato originale   Maestro Nicolò
S. Zeno, Verona   c. 1080*

Mantua to do the great altar triptych. He finished the painting in three years, completing it in 1459. It was the first work of what we call Renaissance painting that anyone in Verona had ever seen. In its spectacular setting it could easily be the first we have ever encountered. Beneath a frieze of Roman putti and brilliantly colored swags of fruit and leaves, the Madonna wears a red dress and a mantle of so deep a blue as to appear almost black. She balances on her knee a truly regal baby boy whose small feet seem to rest on the tips of her fingers. The eight clearly personified saints that surround her look like the original peripatetic philosophers standing in the porches of the Agora in fifth century Athens, only their clothing is brilliantly colored. Peter, Paul, Luke, Zeno, and the Baptist are here keeping company with Mary and the child regnant, although they seem less intent on adoration than enjoying each other's intellectual companionship in a hereafter obviously intended for sages and scholars. In subject, composition and detail, the great triptych stands in contrast to the wonderful old building it ornaments. Smiling Saint Zeno's[3] church was introduced to the absolute best of the new world of the Renaissance by the very first painting of the style in Verona. Things could never again be the same.

We walked back toward the center of town up the Corso Cavour and entered the oldest part of the city by passing Porto Borsari, a fine Roman double gateway that was constructed in the reign of the Emperor Claudius, some time around A.D. 50. Well-preserved Roman gateways abound in Verona. Off the north side of the Piazza delle Erbe we came to the Piazza dei Signori which is also known to locals as the "Dante" from the statue of the great poet that rises in its center.

Dante Alighieri spent time in Verona and in many other towns while he was in exile. He was, of course, a Florentine by birth and sentiment as well as a scholar of Bologna, a sometime soldier, and above all a poet. The passion of his youth was spent in distant adoration of the incomparable Beatrice, daughter of Folco Portinari. She was probably about eight and Dante only nine when he first saw her and fell in love so completely, so deeply and so purely that she remained as the goal and guiding light of all of his life thereafter. He probably only spoke to her two or three times (some years after that first beatific vision) and was surely never alone with her. She died when he was twenty-five. A post-Freudian world has no trouble

---

[3]There is an odd red statue of Zeno on the crypt with a great grin on his face. He is the only saint we saw with such a happy expression in all of our stay in Italy. No one seemed able to explain the cause of his mirth, but the Veronese love him for it.

understanding the depth and seriousness of such affinity. Children have always had real love affairs, but this one is transmuted into the stuff of myth by the genius of the man who recorded the endurance of his youthful ardor.[4]

When he grew up, Dante joined the guild of apothecaries to avoid possible designation as a nobleman and thus be excluded from political office in the democratic commune. The interminable and bloody quarreling of Guelphs and Ghibellines, and the Guelph sub-factions of Blacks and Whites, placed him in the position of judging against his own partisans when he spent a term as a magistrate. He had been Ambassador to San Gimignano and to Rome, but his known impartiality undid him when the Blacks emerged victorious as allies of Charles of Valois, who "helped" the city settle its differences. Dante was exiled for the rest of his life in 1302 at the age of thirty seven. Travelling as we did, we met him in cities all over

---

[4]Modern Americans are not alone in needing a guide with the skill of a Virgil to lead them through the intricacies of the text of the great Comedy. There are shelves full of translations and all have explanatory notes. It seems to me that the most lucid and engaging of these commentaries are those of the best of all detective writers, Dorothy L. Sayers. Whether you have met her detective, Lord Peter, among the great bells of *The Nine Tailors* or encountered the author herself as Harriet Vane at Shrewsbury College in *Gaudy Night*, you should get to know this peculiar lady. The final volume of her translation of the Comedy was finished after her death by Barbara Reynolds. The whole is sprightly and intelligible. More important, her two-level annotation of each canto (by poetic theme and historic reference) is much the best and most approachable gloss of the intricate text. It is published by British Penguin in three paperbacked volumes and should stay in print for a while.

northern Italy where he lived in one court or another
and where he wrote the Comedia. Ravenna, Forlì,
Lunigiana and Verona were honored to have him, as were
for a time Treviso, Lucca and Padua, but he never returned to Florence, whose most famous son he remains
to this day.

We took the modern lift to the top of the Torre dei
Lamberti and surveyed the city, both ancient and modern. The intricate S-curve of the Adige was visible although obscured by buildings. The umbrellas in the Piazza delle Erbe market looked like a mushroom garden
below. The great size of the Roman amphitheater was
quite clear. While surveying the snowy mountains on the
far horizon, we had been standing in the campanile next
to a pair of huge old bells, and, realizing that the hour
was about to strike, fled down the stairs to get out of
range.

In the church of Saint Anastasia there is a wonderful
fresco of Saint George and *la principessa* by Pisanello, although a certain amount of the gorgeous costuming has
peeled from the wall. The painting is full of mysterious
detail: huge horses, tiny hanged men, fairyland castles,
wilderness and domestic scenery. I was unable to find out
what it all meant, but the princess is enchanting.

When you enter Saint Anastasia, whatever your faith
may be, it is worth the risk to bless yourself at the holy
water font at the entrance. This great shell-like basin rests
on the hump and shoulders of a deformed little man, one
of two *Gobbi* that adorn the bases of the first two pillars in
the nave. The face of one reminds me of the handlebar

mustached leader of the posse in an old Western; the other looks very much like Charles Laughton as Quasimodo. The hunchback squints up from under brows polished by the affectionate hands of thousands who pat his head and then dip their fingers in his font, bless themselves, and pray that their sins be forgiven. His affliction can be added to the sufferings of Christ to help supply the means of our absolution. The theological correctness is too clear not to take advantage of the proffered indulgence.

We left the Duomo, the Roman theater, a half-dozen other churches, and Juliet's tomb for another day and sought out a quiet bar for a cocktail while we waited out the tumultuous passeggiata that was starting to surge up *Via Mazzini*.

Later we ate at the Trattoria Anastasia where I braved the local fare, cod fish with polenta, while Cathy was served a grilled trout. We had not yet tried the bollito misto, but we saw it served up from a heated cart that evening and resolved to go for it at the next opportunity. The bollito misto is a sort of New England "boiled dinner" in the large, usually consisting of four or five different meats and sausage, typically a round of beef, a tenderloin of pork, a capon, a leg of lamb, and a *zampone* sausage made of a number of spiced meats stuffed in a pig's trotter. Generous slices of each are served with a series of mustards and fruit condiments, the whole being most properly washed down with a bottle of Lambrusco, a dry, slightly *frizante* red wine. It is a little heavy on the protein and surely the sort of thing that would horrify your cardiologist if he found out about it, but while you are in Emilia, at least once, work up a good appetite and don't miss the bollito.

We climbed the long flights to our locanda with some weariness and slept very well.

IX.

TRAINS
Second Class is Fine

THROUGHOUT all of this itinerant passage-making up, down and across the broad flat valley of the Po, we had been travelling on the Ferrovia della Stato, the state railroad known simply as the F.S. We usually checked the timetable at the hotel desk. They all had one, about the size and shape of Pittsburgh's telephone directory. With a little assistance from the clerk, we learned to predict passage time, and departures for any destination up to the Brenner Pass through the Alps and even beyond.

The one universally applauded legacy of Mussolini is that he made the trains run on time and they still do. They run frequently, go everywhere, are clean, and seem governed by their own code of manners. University students (who are often commuters from small surrounding towns) move into a car's first-class section and sprawl until either a conductor or a tourist with a necktie comes to displace them. On the *accelerati* or the *locali*, which make all the possible stops, the sections are identical anyway. The only difference I can fathom is that if no seats were left, the first-class traveller would be able to claim one in the reserved section. Since we were travelling mostly in April and October, and not during the morning rush to work, we never experienced a crowded train. Incidentally, if you look like a first-class passenger (wearing an expensive hat, for example), you are generally treated as one, not questioned if you use the first-class waiting room and so on.

All the trains are electric powered by overhead wires along the right-of-way, but not on the sidings that connect with the yards or the secondary routes to factories. In my youth, my two brothers and I owned a set of exceptionally sturdy, heavy steel toy trains by "Buddy-L." I think they were made in England but they might have been German. The tracks were at least double the gauge of American Flyer or Lionel trains and the freight cars of three or four types were enameled bright red. This was not an electric train: you pushed it around the iron track and onto the turntable in front of a huge three-chambered roundhouse. We had four or five pieces of rolling stock, hopper car, gondola, flatcar, and caboose, all of which seemed quite realistic when I was eight, even though they were the European single-axle sort of wagons. But the engine was always a disappointment to me. It just didn't resemble the huge, brawny, 4-6-4 steam locomotives that I saw pulling trains through New Milford,

Connecticut in the 1930s. Buddy-L had foisted off on us a dark green vehicle that looked rather like the engine hood and cab of a semi-trailer rig set on steel wheels. Now, at last, I understood and forgave them a lifetime of doubting their integrity. The diesel powered switching engines of all those small Italian towns were perfect replicas of the green Buddy-L engine, and most looked to be about the same age.

We have only good things to report of the F.S. Schedules were clear and easy to find. Stations were manned (or often womaned) by people who knew what was going on and communicated it well even when they didn't speak English. On the one occasion that we took a *Rapido* (also known as an E.C.), we found that the restaurant car served us elegantly and with very good food. If it cost more than most lunches, it included a fine *linguine al funghi*, fresh fruit, and, although we ordered wine by the glass, the waiter poured it generously from a newly opened bottle of Verdicchio. For a return to the luxury now lost to our civilization and a stunning contrast with the airlines, you really should schedule a trip or two on a medium-range train with a real dining car.

On the other hand, there are some places in Italy that really require an automobile to approach. I guess there are others that require a saddled mule.

X.

MANTUA
The City by the Lake

W E CAME TO Mantua after a convincing experience with inexpensive lodgings in Verona. Encouraged to try again, we encountered in the city of the Gonzagas the only really grubby overnight accommodation we found in any town in Italy. This was the hotel of no discernable number of stars that the kindly taxi driver had warned us about. In fairness, however, I must admit that the beds were clean and the bath was well-equipped with a generous, if noisily ventilated shower. But a bare foot on the terrazzo floor encountered little areas of granular *polvere* and the top of the armoire provided enough dust to defile the brim of my new Borsalino, carelessly chucked there the night before. The room looked sort of okay, but the stairs and halls seemed to be both neglected and dilapidated. On the ground floor of the building was a restaurant that had been shut down in mid season, with the tables still un-cleared of the final night's service. Perhaps the proprietario had been ill. We survived, but it put a crimp in our enthusiasm for Mantua. Besides, as a group, the Gonzagas seem to have been one of the less likeable families of the Renaissance in Italy. We promised ourselves at the end that we would come back in the future to attend an opera or a concert in the beautiful little Teatro Accademico where Mozart graced the opening night when he was fourteen. A better albergo, perhaps the Broletto, which the Fielding guide speaks well of, would do wonders for my opinion of the Gonzagas.

Mantua is set in a freshwater sea, but land filling has made the city less defensively isolated today than it was in the Renaissance. Although it was never large, it managed to stay independent of either of the greater powers on either side of it, Milan and Venice. The Gonzagas were more crafty than powerful. As they maintained local ascendancy for almost four hundred years, well into the eighteenth century, they entertained a good opinion of themselves. This is the sort of background that allows succeeding generations of aristocrats to acquire an increasingly exaggerated opinion of their own worthiness. While we were walking through the seemingly endless chambers of the palace known as the "apartments," I wondered what use all those rooms could have. I also became increasingly aware of the inevitability of a bloody reaction to such an unbalanced distribution of material well being that was the norm in seventeenth-century Europe. It arrived of course, when revolution and the later "terror" broke out in France a century later. Italy was not spared. Marie Antoinette's sister, Queen of Naples, was hanged in a particularly grisly execution before a howling mob in the time of Bonaparte.

I eventually realized that the layout of the seemingly endless succession of interconnecting rooms was based on the same principles that inspired Albert Speer's architectural designs for the Third Reich. The more rooms you pass through, the more broad stairways you climb and the more decorated corridors you traverse, so much the greater must be the exaltation and worthiness of the marquis, duke, dictator, pope, or cardinal you will be honored to find in the final room. Certainly the later Gonzagas saw themselves as entitled by divine right to live in extravagant splendor, whatever the condition of the peasant class *contadini* who supported all the art and luxury. After all they had a bunch of cardinals in the family and, a bit later, a saint. He was not actually canonized until a few years after the family lost control of the town in 1708, but for most of the seventeenth century, everybody knew that the formal designation was only a matter of time. Named Aloysius, he was a very young Jesuit, not yet ordained when he died while caring for victims of a plague. He was educated, well bred, talented and only twenty-three years old. After his time, the rest of the family continued to commission rococo art and enjoy the best of things in Mantua. For better than a century their conspicuous consumption seems to have been unrelieved by any good works that might have bailed them out of what looks like a sure reservation for a family suite in one of Dante's lower circles.

In fairness, to the earlier Gonzagas, it should be noted that they also hired some world class scholars to educate their young princelings and princesses as well as great artists to paint their portraits. Thus they improved the lot of their fellow man by commissioning some classy art, even if most of it was intended to show how beautiful, rich and powerful they were.

As time went on and decadence progressed, the Gonzagas spent more than they could squeeze out of their peasants. A later Duke had to raise funds by selling the entire lot of paintings collected through the centuries to Charles I of England. After Charles was beheaded by puritans in 1643, they made a neat catalogue of all the pictures and then sold them to the highest bidders in England. Thence, through the happy effect of high British inheritance taxes, they have been passed into the public domain of the great museums.

Andrea Mantegna came to Mantua from his native Padua in 1460 and was set to work decorating some of the earlier rooms of the palace. His *Camera degli Sposi* fresco shows the Marquis Ludovico and his wife, Barbara of Brandenburg, surrounded by children and pets, uncles and aunts, one cardinal, and other lords spiritual and temporal, all standing about on the walls of a small, exquisite room. Mantegna's foreshortening and perspective (especially of the putti in the *trompe l'œil* oculus painted on the ceiling) are brilliantly inventive and were greatly influential with all the artists of the later quattrocento. In that cool and disciplined four-wall fresco, he records the presence of no less that sixteen members of the family as well as various equerries, masters of hounds and mastiffs. It is one of the sights not to miss in northern Italy, even if you make a day trip to Mantua for it alone.

The person who brought the most style and intellectual color to this town was Isabella d'Este. This remarkable young princess married the Marquis Gianfrancesco Gonzaga, who is depicted as the smaller of the two little boys in the fresco. Francesco took over from his older brother Ludovico. His bride first found him to be something of a boor, but when he left her alone to govern in his place while he acted as Captain General of the armies for the Signory of Venice, she turned out to be shrewd in government as well as a loyal and loving wife. Her letters are the very model of Renaissance correspondence. She was described by everyone as virtuous and wise, even though she was totally convinced that her own pleasure could be defined as the public good. She read Latin as well as Italian and knew some Greek. Her demand that Aldus Manutius print beautiful and scholarly books lead to some of the greatest works of the Aldine Press. Her secretaries filed away her papers and all of her letters to her sister Beatrice and her sister-in-law, Elizabetta Gonzaga, Duchess of Urbino as well as everybody else in Renaissance Italy: warriors, poets, painters and popes. Five hundred years later the letters make good reading. Castiglione, Pietro Bembo, Niccolò Machiavelli and the Bellini boys were among her correspondents. Mantegna was on her household staff; kings, popes and princes sought her esteem. Thus, before the later decadence set in, Mantua was a court of liberal learning and good government while ruled by a woman.

Isabella's portrait was painted by most of the great artists of the late fifteenth and early sixteenth centuries.

Isabella d'Este   Marchesa di Mantova

In an age before *paparazzi,* the essential public relations of government was much enhanced by copious portrait painting. Other nobles, and even the pope would request a portrait of a powerful lady such as the Marchesa of Mantua. She was usually happy to oblige but unfortunately most of these paintings have disappeared or been destroyed in subsequent sieges, sacks, or bankruptcies. Only a charcoal sketch by Leonardo, a medallion by Christoforo Romano, and a painting in full court dress by Titian seem to have survived. This last, which represents her in the full bloom of her beauty, was done when she was over sixty years old, but Titian had a youthful portrait by Francia to work from. Like so many items of the Gonzaga collection, Titian's painting is no longer in Italy but in Vienna. It shows her as she wanted to be remembered.

Being an intellectual and a beauty were not Isabella's only roles. Time and again she pawned her jewels with the bankers of Venice to finance her husband's political and military career, and especially in pursuit of a cardinal's hat for his brother. Once, when he asked her to provide more of such collateral, she reminded him gently that all of her adornments were already engaged with the bankers of Venice except for the two or three items he had given her as wedding presents. But, she added, if their hazard were necessary for his welfare, she would sacrifice not only them but all of her bejeweled costumes, even if she had to appear before him, her Lord husband, "in my chemise."

Mantegna was old when Isabella arrived in Mantua. He died in 1506 at the age of seventy-five and although he seems to have produced little under her patronage, she bargained hard for his Roman bust of *Faustina* for her collection when the artist was old, sick, poor, and beset by debts. She got it from him by promising to stand as guarantor for one hundred ducats owed to his most fierce creditor. Isabella's comments about his death in her correspondence seem curt and perfunctory. At the time she was negotiating for a madonna by one of Mantegna's brothers-in-law, either Giorgio or Giovanni Bellini, I cannot remember which. There was a plague going on, she was pressed for money herself, and her husband was out of town at a war. Still, it seems a pity she did not have the old man cared for more generously. She did, however, advance the career of Raphael's pupil, Giulio Romano. Her son Federico started the Palazzo del Te, down by the lake after she bought up a good part of the old waterfront to convert into gardens and a site for the building. It is an amazing place in spite of having been inundated several times in past centuries to a depth of five or six feet, with the expected effect on the lower parts of the frescoed walls. Today the whole palazzo is a museum and houses travelling exhibits ranging from the Etruscans to the moderns and presents lectures about them. It also has amazing rooms painted with giants, collapsing worlds, and the beginnings of the baroque sensibility.

Among Isabella's most valued acquisitions was a cupid thought to be a Roman antique. It was later discovered to be the work of an almost unknown young sculptor by the name of Michelangel Buonarrotti. Self-centered and tough though she may have been, the lady had a pretty good eye for talent.

After a long day in the palaces of Mantua we sought to compensate for the roughness of our lodgings by seeking out a modestly extravagant ristorante for supper. A cheap room both deserves a good dinner and makes one affordable. We eventually located the White Griffin, where we stopped to make a prenotazione before returning to the sad albergo for a wash and a rest after having walked over half the town. The reservation was a nice gesture, both for us and for the house, but there weren't more than four other couples there during the evening. The headwaiter spread us around nicely to give each an air of being special and the restaurant an air of being occupied. I can't remember precisely what we ordered but I think we began with a *risotto* and went on to a brace of baby salmon. With a *Pinot Grigio* from Friuli, the repast did much to restore our good feelings about Mantua.

XI.

CRIME IN ITALY
Probably No Worse Than What You Are Used To

WE DID NOT experience theft, mugging, hold up, swindle or con job in any of our trips to northern Italy. Our first visit to Rome, however, featured an encounter with a group of gypsy pickpocketing girls and an unknown perpetrator (probably a very young one) who broke a window in our rented car. Many Italians told us the South is where most of the crime occurs in the country. Surely Sicily is the home court of the *Cosa Nostra*, the self-given name of the Mafia, but the Mafia isn't organizing to eliminate the tourist trade just now; they have too many other things on their plate to contend with.

Encounter with an outlaw is something that makes Americans (especially senior Americans) uncertain about travelling in a foreign country without guide or escort. We have concluded that in northern Italy at least, there is less street crime than we are used to in America. In Rome and the South it may be different, which is one reason we put off visiting there until we were better at speaking the language and reading the local climate. We felt very safe in Tuscany, Emilia, Lombardy, Venice, and Umbria.

Concerning violent attack on your person, the possibility of encountering a killer, or at least one who might kill you, is extremely remote and nearly non-existent if you take the minimal precautions you would follow in New York or Boston. We noted that there seem to be very few "drive-by" shootings. Italians have a much, much harder time laying their hands on guns of any sort than do Americans. They are simply not for sale in the stores. Hunting shotguns, mostly single chambered, are around in the country, but the twenty-year-old unemployed city kid almost never has one. Handguns are so expensive and strictly controlled that only the successful and gainfully employed would be likely to have one. This doesn't mean that Italians don't shoot, strangle or stab each other; it means that they don't often do these things with strangers.

In his exuberant book *The Italians,* Luigi Barzini points out that Italians have a considerable fear of sudden death themselves, but the reasons for this anxiety are quite predictable:

> The vigorous passions of a turbulent and restless people are always ready to flare up unexpectedly like hot coals under the ashes. Italy is a blood-stained country. Almost every day of the year jealous husbands kill their adulterous wives and their lovers;

about as many wives kill their adulterous husbands
and their mistresses; fathers or older brothers kill
the seducers of defenseless and guileless virgins, virgins kill the men trying to rape them; desperate
young lovers commit suicide together in pairs, or
separately one at a time. This steady massacre, inspired by love, which has been going on for centuries, has surely cost more lives than the many pes-
tilences and catastrophes which have ravaged the
country, and the wars fought on Italian soil.

Tourism is thus far less dangerous in Italy than a love
relationship or a family tie. Newspapers report a few spectacular crimes wherein the world of vice pays its debts
with strangling scarf or stiletto. Prostitutes and their pimps
often do each other in, and an occasional irate taxpayer
takes on a tax collector. There are more than a few earthquakes, but these can happen in California and, as far as
the rest of America is concerned, tornadoes and hurri-
canes hardly ever happen.

So, barring the collapse of the surface of the planet
in the area you are visiting, there is a simple rule that will
keep you in the statistically safest fraction of the population: avoid romantic entanglement with anyone of either
sex or of any age, except your own dear spouse and your
personal safety will increase by a large factor. If you travel
with your significant other, you will almost surely be safer
than if you go it alone.

As it turns out, usually the only criminals the tourist
has to be on the lookout for are (1) the pairs of athletic

young bag snatchers on Vespas or other *motorini*, and (2) children between the ages of nine and twelve.

The first type cruises the crowded and narrow streets of the busier parts of Rome and Naples with the grabber on the back of the motorino, while the pilot threads his way through the pedestrians looking for a likely tourist's handbag carried over the outboard shoulder. When the rider grabs one, the pilot roars off and is soon around the corner and out of sight. The best defense is to keep the handbag strap over both head and shoulder on the building side of the sidewalk. As a pair, it makes sense for a woman with such a bag not to walk on the curb side.

The second type of street theft is more common and easier to deal with if you are prepared. The culprits are frequently the Gypsy children, often preadolescent girls, who approach from the front holding up a newspaper or a picture as if to show you something of interest. While the paper is in front of your line of sight, the other girls circle to the rear and two or three together will simultaneously pick your pockets. It happens very quickly. The first time I was approached by these children I was surprised, but instinctively shot my left hand into my inner breast pocket to secure my wallet. In the pocket I found the hand of a child which I managed to grasp by the fingers and extract. Twisting a little girl's fingers with one hand while gripping my wallet with the other seemed such an unlikely thing for a sixty-five-year-old grandfather to be doing that I let her go with a great shout while my wife whacked at her with a short, furled umbrella. After it was all over, the street vendors of post cards (we were close to the Colosseum) gave encouraging shouts of outrage, but we noted that they had given no sign of warning when they saw the little gypsy band approach us. We learned that if a child approaches with a picture, magazine, or newspaper in hand, glare, growl, be ready to spit, and shove the tyke away before he or she gets within pocket reach. A savage response to the most innocently childish face is a wise precaution.

Another variation of street pilfering is the helpful bystander who notices that someone just smeared mustard from a sandwich on your coat. Offering to help wipe it off with a Kleenex or handkerchief is a setup for picking your pocket. We resolved to be firm and even impolite in the face of such kindness to keep our distance.

Beyond this, we knew that we should not walk in deserted quarters of any city at night.[1] We also learned to leave nothing in the rental car. Locking an empty car up tight invites breaking into it, and, since it is a rental, theft of the whole car is not an insuperable problem. I once parked on the Aventine Hill in Rome while painting a watercolor sketch of the Tiber below. Forty minutes later, I came back to find the right rear window of the Panda broken, and the canvas cover of the luggage trunk cut open. The only thing missing was a box of Perrugino Bacci, chocolate kisses wrapped in silver paper we were

---

[1] An exception to this is Venice, where it seems perfectly safe to wander about in the dark alleys between buildings and along the sides of the back canals. If there is crime in Venice, we saw no sign of it and almost no policemen.

planning to bring home to our own children. Once again the preadolescent *banditi* had struck.

Precautions against pickpockets are easy to make. My wife wore a necklace wallet with a stainless steel chain underneath her turtleneck travelling blouse. The little leather portfolio was just large enough for her passport, a couple of credit cards and some folding money. Upscale leather goods shops in the U.S. carry them.

Money belts also work, but my own method is slightly more elaborate and more comfortable. I had a tailor make four-by-eight-inch vertical pockets that could be secured to the inside of my trouser waistband with three buttons. My passport case with credit cards, large denomination bills and air line tickets go down inside the belt, inside the trousers, into the deep pocket where they can be gotten at by me alone, with some difficulty at that. I carry some ready cash in a smaller billfold in my inside jacket pocket. So far we have never been robbed of anything while in Italy, except for that one pretty box of chocolates.

Italy has at least four different police forces, and I suspect there are others with still more gorgeous uniforms that I am not familiar with. The local traffic cops are *vigili urbani,* a large number of whom speak pretty good English. A special force for financial crime and counterfeiting whose title escapes me are in evidence at the portals of large banks and are well armed. The *polizia urbana* is the local anticriminal force. The *carabinieri,* a division of the army that carries submachine guns as well as 9mm. pistols, are the elite of law enforcement. They are almost always seen in pairs, and look threatening but always seemed to turn a smiling face toward us. Most speak pretty good English. Venice and other port towns also have a considerable presence of the Coast Guard or *Guardia Costiera*, but we decided we would not ever get to meet them unless we came in our own boat.

We learned the words to shout *"Ladro! Ladro! Aiutarmi! Polizia!"* just in case. But we also learned not to worry about it any more than we would at home in Conneticut or North Carolina.

XII.

MODENA
Home of Ferrari, Maserati and Pavarotti

MANY OF THE larger churches of Emilia-Romagna have lion porches, but those of Modena were the first and are still the most charming. Lovers sit beside them on the sunny south side of the cathedral in autumn, children ride them like pet St. Bernards, tourists photograph them, passing townspeople caress their heads on their way in or out of church. They are present at both the main and the two south side doorways as well as inside where they hold up a splendid rood screen that dates from the late 1190s.

The campanile, which is free-standing off the north corner of the building, is a mighty spire called *la Ghirlandina*, the little garland or wreath, an affectionate diminutive that refers to a bronze wreath on the weathervane which is almost three hundred feet above your head as you stand in the square. The tower is visible for miles around and very much the symbol of the town. It was completed in 1310, and is another of those heroic feats of medieval engineering and architecture that make me wonder if we have really learned much of anything new since the fourteenth century. Inside we noted that the ceiling arches actually function as trusses rather than the barrel vaults and groins more common in the period.

WEST PORCH - MODENA

As a whole, Modena's duomo is the best example of Lombard Romanesque architecture we encountered. Lanfranco, who designed it, was an innovator and his patroness, Contessa Matilda of Canossa, gave him plenty of room to experiment. The twelfth-century sculptor Wiligelmo and his students decorated the exterior in the chaste Lombard style of their time. The carvings appear to grow on the stone supporting members, making this as good an example of integrated design, detailing and decoration as you will ever see. I'd say that Modena's Duomo is right up there with the nearly contemporary Durham Cathedral in Yorkshire as a candidate for "best building."

We came to Modena[1] feeling in need of slightly better quarters than we had the past several nights. We reserved at a three star hotel with a disproportionately modest tariff, the Libertà, on the Via Blasius in the block immediately north of the duomo. It turned out also to have its own garage. Although we didn't need it we made note of its presence, since very few of the hotels in the old town centers have secure parking for cars. The Libertà also had very modern beds, color TV, contemporary furnishings in the lobby, bar and breakfast room. Even the plumbing was right up to date.[2] The train trip was short,

---

[1] The name of the town is one of the many exceptions to the generalization that Italian names are accented penultimately. The stress is on the first syllable.

[2] The Italians can design anything to look wonderful, but function does not always follow form. Most showers rain alike upon the just and the unjust, often unconfined by curtains and seldom possessed of a tile sill which is high enough (if present at all) to keep the water from flowing freely about the room. Toilets are usually of the sort that wash everything down with a mighty jet of high-pressure water but do not provide a bowlful until the handle is flexed. As a result, even the simplest relief of the bowel requires attentive and vigorous scrubbing with the long handled brush provided in a soggy holder in the corner. I do think that a people possessed of such elegant engineering and craftsmanship could do a little better in this regard.

and, since we arrived in the middle of the day, we set out
to scope out the cathedral early in the afternoon.

Later, when we checked the news, we saw a sorrow-
ful anchor reporting what the newspapers had been printing for several days: Federico Fellini was gravely ill and
seemed to be sinking.

The Harvard guidebook recommended Trattoria Da
Omer just across the parklet near the Libertà. We got a
reservation through the good offices of the desk clerk,
but we didn't realize how early one must book at the
Omer. It is an inexpensive and very popular place to enjoy Emilian food. Signora Omer was manning the cassa
when we arrived. She was tying little knots in the hand-
made tortellini when we arrived. She also welcomed her
guests, brought the menu, served the wine, and waited
on tables. Her husband, who did all the cooking, was
tangentially visible in his immaculate whites and gleaming kitchen. I think they had a pot walloper out in back
to do the dishes, but other than that it was strictly a family affair. We were served a plate of just three large, plump
ravioli containing a collection of rare cheeses, under a
pale pink Emilian sauce with a colorful garnish of thinly
sculptured red and green bell pepper. It was just about as
delicious as anything I have ever eaten. For a secondo we
had some mysterious and ambrosial pork slices and spinach that had been brought to worthy attention by quite a
lot of garlic and a trace of the famous Modenese balsamic
vinegar.

After that first experience we tried to go back the
following night, but we couldn't get in. If you go there,

reserve early for the following night just to be sure. We noted in an older edition of the Harvard guide- book that a "heart-wrenching depiction of Adam and Eve being evicted from the Garden of Eden" was to the left of the main door of the Cathedral. We stopped to study it, having become affezionati of such scenes from our other experiences in Verona, Orvieto and Bologna. Modena's expulsion is first-class twelfth-century depic- tion in stone, but to my mind is surpassed by the horror of Cain bashing Abel over the head with an enormous truncheon in the neighboring panel. This is the same work that was presented to the youthful vision of Jacopo della Quercia as he wrestled with his vision of Greeks and Romans, fusing them in the amazing creation panels at San Petronius.

The major museums of Modena are happily gath- ered together in the *Palazzo dei Musei* where the remain- ing treasures of the Estense are housed.[3] I think the last of the family may have sold some of the art work to British

---

[3] We wondered how the Este collection got from Ferrara to Modena. The family had some ups and downs after the lovely daughters of Duke Ercole I made their spectacular marriages. By 1598, an illegitimate greatgrandson of Lucrezia Borgia and Alfonso Este became duke. The pope refused to recognize him, and, having at the time a sizeable army, took control of Ferrara. As usual the emperor was on the outs with the papacy, and made the young man Duke of Modena. His name was Cesare and he moved the entire family into the new duchy, where they stayed up to the time of the American Civil War. It took something like six hundred baggage wains to carry the art work and furniture to their new castle. Amazingly, their secretaries and notaries managed to defy the old adage that "two moves are as good as a fire," and kept the entire archive of political negotiations, kitchen bills, military treaties, social correspondence, and sisterly letters together and it still exists either in Ferrara or Modena.

and American millionaires in the nineteenth century, but there is still lots of painting, armor, ceramics and archeological treasure trove in Modena. We spent a number of happy hours in the various museums and innocently asked where we could see the Borso d'Este, not knowing whether it was a pocketbook or an early form of stock exchange.[4] A most obliging librarian got out a bunch of keys and led us through the study rooms of a contemporary library to a showcase that contained the most marvelous manuscript we have ever seen. This Bible, for such it turned out to be, was made in the late fifteenth century, just as printing was beginning to replace illuminated manuscripts, if indeed the Borso is really the product of hand lettering. The brilliant execution of the text seems almost too regular to have come from the pen of a scribe. Of one thing there is no doubt, the illuminations done by Taddeo Crivelli are wonderworks of the illuminators art. Saints, dragons, sea shells, flowers and abstract designs frame each page. Huge uncial initials on each chapter or paragraph are decorated with gilded backgrounds, fantastic arabesques, paisley shapes and flowers. The librarian was proud to show it off.

Later, while exploring the church of San Pietro, we were beckoned by a young verger to view the paintings in the sacristy, the room in which the priests put on their vestments before mass or other ceremonies. The process

---

[4] I discovered later that Borso d'Este was a person, the member of the family who commissioned the Schifanoia palace in Ferrara as well as the famous Bible.

of vesting is surrounded by ceremony and prayer, especially in the case of bishops who even have special prayers
for putting on their white shoes. To keep the good pa-
dres' minds on track, vestries are required to have a crucifix on display, and in many cases the entire room is lav-
ishly decorated with religious art. In some churches the
greatest paintings were thus hidden away in this private
location; perhaps not a bad idea if they served to get the
reverend cranked up for a good homily.

The verger told us there would be a short organ re-
cital in a few minutes, and that the organ dated from
1525. He gave us plenty of time in the sacristy, and when
we returned to the church he locked the door behind us
and then went to the nave to welcome a pair of young
visitors who seemed to be waiting for him. There were
embraces, greetings and a moment's happy talk in rapid
Italian. He then switched on some lights that showed off
a magnificent organ front above our heads and disappeared
up a stair to the tracker keyboard, hidden in the gallery of
the instrument. He had not told us that he was the or-
ganist as well as the verger and probably sexton as well.
The mighty old pipes made the building echo with J.S.
Bach for about three-quarters of an hour. We and the
young couple were his only audience. He spoke excellent English, played very well indeed, and collected CDs
of Anthony Newman. We told him that we would intro-
duce him if he ever got to the United States and, attempting to feel a little like Renaissance patrons of a young
artist, forced him to accept a few thousand Lira notes to
get him started on saving for the airfare.

We had a full day of museums, music and walking about the center of the town. We dined in the second-floor trattoria, Da Enzo, run by the same family that owned the hotel and not far from the success of the night before. We finally abandoned all that my cardiologist recommended and ordered the bollito misto we had been observing in Emilian restaurants for some time. The selections included tongue, *zampone*, beef, capon, calves head, and *cotechino* sausage. I commanded a bottle of lambrusco, the light, fizzy red wine that is requisite with such fare. Although my wife found it less enchanting, I felt that it cut through the weight of the meat with great success. With all the condiments it was not exactly a light supper, but then, think of the educational experience.

If the food of Emilia-Romagna is a trifle rich at times (I mean these people sometimes put butter on their thinly sliced ham!), the drink provided is light. Northern Italian wines aren't always easy to find in the U.S., and although we all know Chianti and Soave, even these will offer some pleasant novelty when tasted in their home court. White wines like Est!Est!Est!, Prosecco, Orvieto, Verdicchio, and Pinot Grigio may be new experiences for you. We combined our practice of drinking mostly white wine (saving the reds like Valpolicella for game and Bolognese Ragù) with the Italian custom of having wine with at least two of the three meals of the day. But Italians are moderate in the amount of wine they drink at any one time. We adopted their pattern of ordering a half-liter of *acqua minerale* along with a half-liter of the house white at lunch. The local wines were almost always delightful and a great bargain. We occasionally asked a nice waiter to pick out a bottle for us, giving him a price range to work from. This is how we discovered Est!Est!Est!, a semi-*secco* of Tuscany.[5] Even small restaurants stock several brands of mineral water, with San Pelegrino being perhaps the most popular. We usually took whatever the house offered; they all seemed very good to us. We liked the sparkling variety (*gasata*) but you can also have it without bubbles (*normale*) if you wish.

Getting back late to the Libertà we switched on the television to check on the world as we got to bed. The scene was familiar, from an old movie that at first I did not recognize. And then we realized it was from *Amarcord,* Fellini's gentle and most autobiographical masterpiece of the 1960s. We knew at once that he must have died, and thought that a few clips of his films were being used to illustrate the newscast. But no, the scenes went on until it all reeled again before us: Uncle Matthew being coaxed

---

[5]The name comes from a story of the eleventh century. The Cardinal Archbishop of Augsburg was going to Rome, surely for some serious ecclesiastical reason. He sent his steward ahead to reconnoiter the inns along the way, marking those with good wine in chalk with Est! (It Is!). When the Bishop got to Montefiascone, near Viterbo but well short of Rome, he came upon an inn marked with the word three times, followed by a series of exclamation marks. Entering, he discovered his servant, quite unconscious with a blissful smile on his face. Impressed, the Bishop called for a stoup of the best vintage. He drank so much that he too passed out, but, unfortunately never came to and was buried in the village of Montefiascone where he still lies. Both the wine and its source are still there too, the temporary chalk designation having been made the permanent name of the inn as well as the vintage.

down from the tree by the midget nun; the woman news vendor with the enormous bosom and the adolescent boy; the lovers separated by the heaped-up walls of snow which were shoveled from the paths in the cathedral square. All the other programming had been canceled to air it as a memorial to Fellini. For the next several days the newspapers and the TV were largely devoted to mourning the loss of *nostro* Federico. All of the magazines we saw on the airplane flying home several weeks later devoted most of their space to him. He was a friendly hero to all Italians, a beloved relative who understood them and of whom they could be justly proud.

We left Modena without visiting either of the hot rod automobile factories or seeing the Ferrari museum of bright red cars. But we loved this town: even the quality of hotel was superior to its rating. We found that like the cars, everything—tenors, art, music, film, history, food— all are world class in Modena.

XIII.

CARS AND THEIR PILOTS
The Song of the Open Road

THE ITALIANS have always made the most beautiful and fastest cars in the world. The Bugatti of the late 1930's was a legendary vehicle, streamlined more elegantly than any other of its era. The Ferrari and the Maseratti are surely among the most expensive and beguiling toys available to the richest, most discriminating drivers today. But Italians don't exactly drive a car. Their word is *guidare,* which is something both more and less than our *drive.* The verb suggests that the magnificent machine, from the tiniest Fiat to the Lancia and Lamborghini, is having its own way with the road, scorching the pavement to its own pleasure. The happy owner behind the wheel is giving it guidance, perhaps urging it on to ever greater feats of power, speed and traction. But the intention, the will and the desire are in the body and soul of *la macchina.*

It is said by some statisticians that while the Italians
have the greatest number of recorded accidents per hundred thousand kilometers driven in Europe, they have a
much lower number of fatalities than most other countries.[1] This may have something to do with the way in
which statistics are compiled. The Germans and Swedes
are ashamed of their accidents, but the Italians flaunt their
record of bent fenders and crumpled bumpers as a badge
of honor.

1939 BUGATTI   3.3 litre coupé

And they maintain their cars in gleaming perfection
if they are anywhere near new. They treat them with almost reverential respect as honored guests of the family.
It is as though the Italian, when taking a surrogate mistress in the form of a 172-CV Turbo, prefers to treat her
with the dignity and respect one should accord to a countess, or at least a lady of noble lineage. Washed, waxed,
polished and gleaming in brilliant red or glossy black, she
is something between a duchess and a strumpet and her
fidanzato is head over heels in love with her.

Unlike the Autobahnen of Germany, there are more

---

[1] The Portuguese are reputed to be the deadliest drivers.

or less binding speed limits on the great *autostrade* that
connect the major cities of the peninsula. The roads are
wonderfully engineered, and have reduced travelling time
between north and south from days to hours. They are
safe, swift and pleasant driving, even if they stay away
from the picturesque and populated towns along the way.
But most of us are not ready, at least initially, to maintain
a pace that will keep us out of the way of a happy Italian
driver, inevitably male and probably a descendant of one
of those halberdiers that Pontormo painted. He approaches
from the rear at 125 kph while we are lazing along at
what seems a breathtaking clip in the lefthand lane of the
superhighway. His high-beam headlights start to flash on
and off in the noonday light as he approaches. He will
not sound his horn until well upon you, so keep an eye
out for those flashing lights. These signals, which would
be taken as a sign of some hostility in the U.S., are nothing of the sort here. He knew that we wanted to move
over before he arrived on our rear bumper and he was
merely giving a cheery salute, with thanks for not inhib-
iting his pleasure or forcing him to reduce speed. This
meaning of the flashing lights becomes quite clear on the
good secondary roads where there are but two lanes separated by a bright yellow stripe. Stay with the game, keep
your speed, but when you see those lights, edge slightly
to the right and leave four or five feet available to your
companion from the rear. That's all he will need. Flashing
brightly to the oncoming traffic, he will straddle the yellow line and pass while the cars in the oncoming lane
make a similar shrug of an accommodation to allow him

through without ever meeting another vehicle head on.

This is such an expected procedure that I soon got accustomed to it (the two-lane roads are often quite wide), and I knew that sooner or later I would try it myself. From that liberating moment onward, I was no longer the timid patsy that I was when I left the Avis lot at Malpensa Airport. Like Mr. Toad in *The Wind in the Willows*, I too became the Lord of the Open Road, the Terror of the Highway. Off with a cheery wave to those we passed, I found myself happily flashing my headlights at the guy in front, who was dawdling along at 100 kph, just before I dashed on between him and the gleaming diesel Mercedes fourteen-wheeler that was coming the other way down the two-lane strip.

In adopting this local style of guiding a car, however, you should be equipped with something a touch more battle-ready than the Fiat *Panda* or the Ford *Festiva*. These little fellows are wonderful cars and much the cheapest to charter, but rapid acceleration is not one of their great virtues. And the ability to go from 80 to 120 kph without a lot of gear changing when trying to retreat to the right hand lane if caught short for space, is one of the essentials of the Italian style of pleasure driving.

At least Italians drive from the "proper" side of the car and on the usual U.S. side of the road. This makes it a lot easier to get used to than the classic case of going through an English roundabout and winding up, after making a left turn, full in the teeth of the oncoming traffic. In Italy the cars stay more or less on the side of the road you are expecting them to use. I took up driving in

Italy at the age of 64 and found that my eyes and reflexes were perfectly adequate to the demands made upon them. I even got an "International" drivers license, which is a sort of racket of the automobile clubs: $10 for a permit that has to be renewed *every* year. We were also deceived by the well kept secret of the V.A.T. (Value Added Tax), which is seldom quoted up front in the rental advertisements. It was 18 percent when I last looked and might be 20 percent, by now, thus making a considerable difference. Renting in advance from the big U.S. agencies provided a special rate, but the V.A.T. appeared on the credit card statement a month after we got home. Fuel is expensive, but most European cars are real gas misers. Some rental agencies will supposedly help you find low cost tourist coupons for *benzina* as a government subsidy to help the tourist business. We were unable to find any.

We enjoyed touring by rail and car in turn. The great advantage of the automobile is that it makes the hill towns, country monasteries and outlying Palladian farm houses accessible. We discovered a most marvelous lunette of the Virgin and Child by Luca della Robbia over a courtyard doorway in a very obscure monastery along a country road south of Florence. On the same trip we bought a spit-roasted chicken from the itinerant proprietor of a canteen truck in the square of San Gimignano. It provided a fine picnic from the tailgate of the car when we stopped by the side of a canal that tumbled over a small waterfall.

XIV.

RAVENNA
Christianity and Civilization in a Dark Age

Ravenna today seems to be an ordinary place with extraordinary things in it. The old town is small and ringed by petrochemical factories. It is far surpassed in population by the beach towns a dozen miles to the east, where the sea went when it deserted this late Roman city and withdrew.

The shifting sands of this part of the Adriatic were the cause of both the rise and decline of Ravenna. The town was naturally protected by impassible swamps when Rome began to look less secure from both the voracious crowds within the city and the surging barbarians to the north. As a result, later emperors (most of whom had only a shaky grasp on the purple) began to spend more and more time at what must originally have been a kind of imperial resort. Finally, Honorius, after trying Milan

as a capital and discovering he was even more in the path
of visiting barbarians, moved the whole executive structure of government to Ravenna in 404, leaving what was
left of the Senate behind to shift for itself. That was just
about in the nick of time, since Alaric took Rome in
410.[1] Less than a century later, the Ostrogoths were lords
of the Empire, and they used Ravenna as their capital.

But between the mid-fifth and sixth centuries,
Honorius' sister, Galla Placidia, and the later Gothic king
Theodoric, gave their minds and treasure to things of the
spirit. This other-worldly Christianity was somewhat divided between Arian and Orthodox communions but
unified by the most amazing works of mosaic to be found
anywhere in the world.

---

[1] Alaric has gotten bad press through the years, some of it undeserved. He
had been an officer in the Roman Army and was a Christian. The Roman
Army was full of hired Goths, the Emperor was not exactly a square shooter,
and when Alaric changed sides, lots of the army came with him. As a
sacker of cities he did a mild job on Rome, not a patch on the *real* sack that
took place when the Christian Constable of Bourbon, part of the entourage
of the H.R.Emperor Charles V, brought down an army of mercenaries
from virtually every country north of the Alps. He died of a crossbow bolt
that Benvenuto Cellini claimed to have fired. The year was 1527. There
being no orders from the the distant Emperor, and no one in charge of the
army, the soldiers, having taken the city, settled down to ten or eleven
months of occupation during which murder and rape, arson, looting, and
the torture of those who might have hidden valuables, set a record
unsurpassed even by the Serbian militia men of our own time. Compared
to the young fellows of Charles V's army, Alaric, and even Genseric who
did quite a job on the town in 455, could be considered minor league
Rome sackers.

There are two baptistries in Ravenna: one orthodox at the cathedral and the other free-standing, known as the Arian Baptistry. An oversimplified differentiation between these two types of Christianity goes roughly this way: Arians (who were trying to use human reason to relate what they believed of Jesus to what they believed of God) felt that while Christ was unique, he was not eternal since he was begotten of God the Father. The difference between *genetos,* "made" and *gennetos,* "begotten" is frightfully important even though recorded by a single doubled letter and perhaps hard to hear at all in declamation. Most of the "we believe this, but not that" sort of definition in the early stanzas of the Nicene Creed come from the fathers attempting to settle this sort of thing back around 325 when the Emperor Constantine forced the arguing factions on one of the issues to accept the term "consubstantial," or *homoousios,* to define the relationship of the persons of the Trinity. All of this was very serious stuff in the fourth century, and it still is in some quarters today. Lots of heads were broken over questions of hypostatic union. What is known as the "filioque" clause helps to maintain the enmity of the Croats and the Serbs today.

By the time of the flowering of Ravenna, the Goths were still Arian and the somewhat more Roman population was orthodox. Some signs of this difference can be deduced from the great mosaics of the two baptistries. The orthodox apostles, the stuccoed figures of prophets and the dove of the Holy Spirit have a familiar look to them to western eyes. John the Baptist is pouring water from a hand-held shell rather than pressing Christ down for total immersion, a detail some think is due to later restoration.

In the Arian baptistery, which was built by Theodoric fifty years later than the orthodox one (around the year 500), the image of Christ came as a shock to us. He is depicted in a brilliant mosaic as a young man, naked and beardless, standing half-submerged in the water, his Jewish masculinity clearly defined by circumcision. The Baptist's hand is on his shoulder, ready to submerge him. John looks a little anxious, obviously aware that this is no ordinary penitent, but a very human one nonetheless. The Spirit, in the form of a dove, pours water from its beak upon the Lord's head, a detail which fits with the prophecy from the Book of Joel:

> I will pour out my Spirit upon all flesh;
> And your sons and daughters shall prophesy,
> Your old men shall dream dreams,
> Your young men shall see visions; . . .
> In those days I will pour out my spirit.

The colored tesserae of the mosaics are either stone, ceramic, or covered with gold leaf. They are as brilliant today as when they were assembled fifteen centuries ago.

Theodoric commissioned his own tomb before his death in 526. The building, reminiscent of Hadrian's tomb in miniature, is dodecahedral and made of Istrian stone from the far northern end of the Adriatic Sea near Trieste. It is vaulted over with a single, carved, dome-shaped slab more than thirty feet across and better than a yard thick.

Presumably it was brought to the port of Classe on some raft of wonderfully ample proportion. The monolithic dome is estimated to weigh something like three hundred metric tons, so that raft must have been a monster. I wonder what propelled it? Theodoric's kingdom obviously did not lack either organization or inventiveness. His engineers still remembered the skills of the imperial centuries.

RAVENNA   Theodoric's Tomb
C. 525 A.D.

The older of the two Basilicas of St. Apollinaris is a few miles south of the center of the town in Classe. There was a near war over moving his relics to the other basilica in the town. He was the first bishop of Classe and this, his original resting place, is still used as a place of worship rather than as a museum. Even if its mosaics are less spectacular than the other St. A's, it is a wonderful building from the mid-sixth century. The bishop who ordered it built had the financial backing of Julian the Silversmith, referred to in a contemporary guidebook as "the mysterious and very rich Greek" who almost simultaneously was also paying for the building of Saint Vitalus' basilica back in town. If most of the Roman Empire was deep in the dark in the sixth century, a languidly bright and beautiful spot thrived at Ravenna.

The decoration of the great Basilica of Saint Apollinaris is Arian, having been commissioned by Theodoric in the early sixth century. Christ is once again depicted as young and unbearded, looking like a youthful Roman patrician, although he grows a beard and matures visibly as the sequence of New Testament scenes unfolds. Below the clerestory windows, the upper walls present a seemingly endless file of the blessed, robed in gold and white, and carrying palms in their hands. In that nave you can still feel the security of the rigidly ordered Byzantine civilization hanging on inside its walls, bemused by the theology and the artifice of the East. This is the time that Yeats imagined when he wrote

> Once out of nature I shall never take
> My bodily form from any natural thing
> But such a form as Grecian goldsmiths make
> Of hammered gold and gold enamelling
> To keep a drowsy Emperor awake;

Or set upon a golden bough to sing
To lords and ladies of Byzantium
Of what is past, or passing, or to come.

While all the while the fierce and still destructive
Langobards savaged the countryside to the west and prepared to breach the defences of the town.

XV.

URBINO
The Renaissance Began in the Mountains

THE HILL TOWN of Urbino rates a scant dozen or fifteen line entry in the five feet of shelf space that my encyclopedia occupies. Its name, however, crops up in many other entries about the people, artists, and style of the Italian Renaissance. *Let's Go Italy '93* is less restrained: "If you only visit one town in Italy, make it Urbino."

Getting to Urbino takes a little planning. This is one of the towns we approached in the rented Fiat Panda, which had to be urged over some of the hills in a variety of lower gears. But even Urbino can be gotten to by public transportation by first taking a train down the Adriatic coast to Pêsaro and then one of the ten daily buses that leave from the vicinity of the station. Alternatively, you might get a bus from Assisi and approach from the west. The trip up into the mountains is pretty and you can see the high-turreted cut-out of the little city above you against the sky shortly before you arrive. It is an uphill walk to the center of town but there is said to be an elevator from the *parcheggio* where the buses stop that will take you most of the way. We drove around the base of the town twice searching for a way in. As a university town more than a commercial center, Urbino has a limited number of hotels, but the guidebooks speak well of the Albergo Italia and the Hotel San Giovanni. We stayed at the Bonconte.

Whenever we changed cities, we prevailed upon the desk clerk of our current hotel to make our reservation for two nights hence. This put the least strain on my beginning Italian and seemed to please the clerks. As we found with dinner reservations, the clerks assumed the role with flair and emphasis, usually in a loud voice and very rapid Italian with a sort of upper-class distinctness of speech. Some offered advice about which hotel we should book. One clerk made three calls to find us the sort of room we wanted. He didn't charge us for the calls, but was happy to accept a thousand Lira tip, more I think for the resultant esteem than for its value.

The famous Urbino of the later quattrocento is largely the work of Federico Montefletro, successor to a family of strong men of the Marches who raised the county to the status of a duchy.   He was the illegitimate son of Guidantonio, Count of Urbino, the Captain of the Papal Army, and of Elisabetta degli Accomanducci dei Conti di Petroio of Gubbio. His birth was kept a secret for two and a half years to spare the feelings of the countess, and also to protect the identity of his mother who was much under the age of consent at the time of her seduction. But the countess died in 1423, leaving Guidantonio with an infant heir who was soon killed by enemies of Urbino. He moved swiftly to marry the pope's niece,[1] but that lady, however legitimate, remained childless. With his new wife's consent, the count then recognized the infant Federico as his proper heir. But soon the new countess surprised everybody by becoming pregnant. The resulting possibility for confusion in the line of succession led Guidantonio to send young Federico off to be reared by a widowed lady relative who ruled Sant'Angelo in Vado and Marcatello. To seal the bargain, the little boy was betrothed to her daughter Gentile and thus became heir to that earldom. This was presumably enough of an honor and responsibility to keep him busy and out of competition with his little brother. When he was eleven, having lived in the home of his fiancée for eight years, Federico was used as a hostage to Venice by the pope, and later was shipped to the Gonzaga court in Mantua where he received the best available classical education. When he was sixteen, he finally returned to Gentile who was then twenty-one. They were married in Gubbio. Federico then set out on a brilliant military career. He won all his battles, sometimes by amazing feats of derring-do. He scaled the

---

[1]Papal family relationships are often subject to some historical confusion from the fact that the word nipote can mean either nephew or niece (nipota) as well as grandson or granddaughter. Thus the fault we term "nepotism" could mean appointing any of one's own progeny to a post, not just those of the official's siblings.

overhanging Rock of San Leo to defeat the Malateste,
and was made hereditary Earl of Massa Trabaria by the
pope in 1443.

At his father's death, Federico's younger half-brother
(the fully legitimate one), was declared Count of Urbino
and then made a duke by the pope. He was slain in a
conspiracy the following year. Federico rushed to the town
and arrived during the tumult that followed the murder.
He met with the local magnates and impressed everybody with his intelligence and forcefulness. Soon after,
he was carried triumphantly to the church where he was
proclaimed Count and Lord of Urbino. It took thirty
years before the next of several popes, the numerically
redundant Sixtus the Fifth made him Duke of Urbino
and Gonfalonier of the Holy Roman Church.

Federico Montefeltro
Dux Urbino

I have no record of his succession of wives, although
the documents surely exist. He certainly acquired more
than one. The blond lady in the paired portraits in the
Uffizi painted by Piero della Francesca is not Gentile, but
Battista Sforza of Milan, a lady of even more impressive
monetary endowment. That painting shows off the famous divot in the bridge of Federico's nose. The blemish
is prominent in all of his portraiture because he was always painted in profile, having lost his right eye in the
same jousting accident that took out the chunk of nose.

Federico was perhaps the greatest of that remarkable
class of Italian characters, the *condottiere*, captains of the
mercenary armies that fought the wars of the time. Italy
was largely urbanized in the fourteenth and fifteenth centuries, and even the rural populations surrounding the
cities were not under the feudal obligation of homage to
a lord, a system that provided an easy means of conscrip-
tion of armies in transalpine Europe. Townspeople were
free citizens, and, although they would build walls and
defend them in their own interest, they could not be
readily conscripted and sent to war in the field against a
rival army. The city communes therefore hired small professional armies, contracting with a captain who would
provide troops, men, horses, weapons, and military
knowhow. Federico was not only a master of this profes-
sion, he acquired a justified reputation for fulfilling his
contracts in an age where the double cross was the norm
and alliance usually had to be assured by exchange of treasure and hostages. As a result of his reputation for straight
shooting, he gained the wealth which, coupled with good

taste, enabled him to hire men like Luciano Laurana as his architect and the likes of Piero della Francesca, Paolo Uccello, and Raphael's father, Giovanni Santi as painters.

Federico ran a sort of military school for young noblemen from other parts of Europe and supposedly trained princes from as far away as England in the arts of war. Poets and philosophers were welcome at his court. Many years later, during the reign of the last duke of the line, Baldasarre Castiglione wrote a memorable description of this Italian Camelot in *The Book of the Courtier*, which served as a handbook of politics, manners and diplomacy for the later Renaissance. The Montefeltro

Palazzo Ducale   URBINO

Palacealso seems to have functioned as a postgraduate university, where pursuit of classical language and literature was illuminated by learned discussion and contemporary artists were encouraged to practice painting and architecture. Some commentators have ventured the opinion that the Renaissance as an intellectual movement really began at Urbino.

What with all the climbing, we were happy to slide back down to the wall where we were put up at the friendly Hotel Bonconte in a pleasant room a little removed from the center of the passeggiata of the young and old in the Piazza della Repubblica. A half-hour *pisolino* rallied us for a return to the fray. In attempting to find our inn earlier in the day, we had driven to the summit and somehow passed some stone posts, intended as a checkpoint turning traffic away, to find ourselves in the rear court of a restaurant called Pasta à Gogo. The proprietor was vastly amused by our ability to navigate the little Fiat through the supposedly interdicted streets at the top of the hill. He guided us on a route down to Via della Mura and was even more amused when I translated it as "Wall Street." The downhill course over the slates and cobbles was as breathless as the descent of a forty meter Olympic ski jump, but the brakes held and we found the Bonconte at the bottom of the slope.

In spite of the outdated, faddish name, we found the dinner at Pasta à Gogo delicious and the friendly proprietario helpful and voluble. His selection of a special wine was only moderately pricey and a wonderful experience. We signed the guest book and have received several Christmas and New Year's cards in the ensuing years. Walking back down the steeply sloping stones of the town late at night was an experience totally removed from home. Why we came.

Before leaving Urbino, we discovered the dark side of both medieval and contemporary Europe in a fascinating and well known work of art. One of the most enigmatic paintings of the quattrocento is the set of six little panels from an altar predella by Paolo Uccello. They depict the story of "The Profanation of the Host." Guidebooks and commentators say the scenes show a guilty woman who sells a consecrated communion wafer to a Jewish merchant. For some inexplicable reason (did he *believe* it was true flesh?), he attempts to cook the host in a pan before his fireplace. It runs over with bright blood that seeps under the door of his house and attracts the attention of soldiers, who attack the door with crowbars and axes. The sacrament is restored to the tabernacle in a richly vested procession; the woman is taken out at night to be hanged; the merchant and all his family are burned at the stake, also under cover of darkness. Two pairs of angels and devils wrestle over the body of the woman which is laid out in some dignity in front of the altar.

It is worth noting that this tale of anti-semitic guilt by reputation, and the summary lynching in the darkness, is positioned on an altar supporting the tabernacle, a pious embellishment to accentuate the holiness of the sacrament and to teach reverence for it. Was it based on some actual, horrible witch hunt in the ages before Uccello's own time? Who commissioned it? I like to think that the sympathetic depiction of the merchant is, like

Shakespeare's Shylock, an example of the work of an artist who at least points out the ambiguity of human guilt, even if there is nothing he can do to deflect the near-universal disapprobation or blunt the popular choice of vengeance. Such voices are like that of Justice Blackmun speaking against capital punishment while a chorus of popular politicians cried out for more frequent use of the gas chamber, the electric chair, and the lethal needle.

The woeful face of the woman, gazing piteously upward with the rope already looped around her neck, could not have been done by a painter who did not have compassion for the convicted. I also see nothing in any of the scenes that Uccello intended the merchant to be recognized as a Jew. He has no beard or costume detail that might represent him as such. The painting above his hearth shows the profile of a black, a scorpion, and an *eight*-pointed star. I wonder who first designated the hapless merchant, the host buyer, as a Jew?

The tiny figures on the little panels are brilliant and heartbreaking. Whatever enlightenment has occurred since the quattrocento, assignment of semitic guilt seems still to be present in the modern attribution of unredeemable sin to the religion of the profaner and his wife and children. How many generations are still to be reared on such tales?

XVI.

CORTONA
The Very Acme of the Hill Town

I CAN'T REMEMBER why we determined to visit Cortona. It was on the best route coming back north to Siena after our stop at Urbino, but it wasn't given much space in the guidebooks. They all made mention of it, and the few lines in Michelin were intriguing. We had never heard of it but decided to give it a try.

The town roosts on top of an ancient hill in an upland plain between the watersheds of the Arno and the Tiber. It sits off the left shoulder of the Apennines, within sight of the great bowl of Lake Trasimeno to its south. The lake area attracts vacationers today. Once, more than two thousand years ago, it was the site of one of the major victories of the then seemingly invincible Carthaginians under Hannibal, who had come from Africa through the snowy high-altitude passes of the Alps and descended into Italy. He took the plain of the Po and ravaged his way down the river valleys to this point. It was here that the Romans led by Flaminius stood to wage battle. The augury of swarms of bees settling on the eagles of the Roman standards should have warned them that the day would not go well. Even more significant was the lakeside mist that rose from the osiers and fens. It disguised the presence of Hannibal's cavalry, which was unnoticed in the early fighting and then fell upon the Roman rear. The result was devastating. Rome itself seemed destined to be taken when its army was defeated even more decisively in the subsequent slaughter farther south in Apulia, at Cannæ.

Roman and Carthaginian commentators felt that Hannibal could have destroyed the city on the Tiber within the week if "he had known as well how to use his victory as how to gain it."[1] But Hannibal rested his army still farther south at Capua, where his soldiers "grew soft in luxury" while the Romans made new arms, freed slaves to swell their shattered army, and prepared for his advance. The Roman commander Fabius gave his name to the gradual approach to solving political or social affairs by delaying any decisive conflict.

---

[1] Adherbal, the son of Bomilcar, evidently wrote this, although who saved his writing from the later destruction of Carthage I do not know.

Hannibal stayed in southern Italy for fifteen years, but he never conquered Rome even though he never lost a battle. The Romans jabbed at his supply lines, and eventually Scipio invaded Africa to threaten Carthage itself. Hannibal then packed up his diminished troops and went home.

The wealth of precise information we have about these bloody years (218 to 202 B.C.), and our total ignorance of equally horrible and more decisive events that occurred six or eight centuries later in the same part of the world, makes the period before and after the Roman zenith seem even more obscure by contrast. Who swam or fished in Lake Trasimeno after the soldiers' bodies rotted away? Few were around to bury them.

In Cortona we urged the little car up steep streets to the Piazza della Repubblica, and we were able to look down at the Umbrian plain and the distant prospect of the lake from our pleasant room in the Hotel San Michele. But later we learned that we had hardly scaled the height of Cortona. Walking ever upward on the following day, we reached the Etruscan walls, huge sandstone blocks whose smoothly fitting irregular shapes remind me of the Inca stonework in Peru.

Cortona was first settled by the Umbrians, whoever they were, even before the Etruscans fortified it. It certainly does give the impression of being a very old town, although one of its prettier buildings is a nineteenth-century Romanesque church on the flank of the hill below the town, a shrine to St. Margaret of Cortona who died in 1297, just before the Renaissance broke upon the town.[2]

Cortona, never large, has only room for 20,000 people on top of the hill today and I doubt that it has ever been larger. It was the home of Luca Signorelli whose fantastic crowds of naked figures in murals of the Last Judgement in Orvieto were a prefiguring of Michelangelo's work. His paintings are in the Diocesan Museum. In this collection is yet another Annunciation, this one by Fra Angelico, that my wife ranks at the top of the genre in all of Italy.

Another museum is the Etruscan Academy, a modern continuation of an eighteenth-century intellectual club that numbered Voltaire among its early members. The Etruscans have always exercised a strong pull on the European imagination, both because they were the greatest competition for the early Romans and because we know so very little about them. Their language is still virtually unreadable, their customs mysterious, and their origins

---

[2] Margaret is styled a "concubine" in the terminology of the church, although we might classify her as more of a mistress today. At least she doesn't seem to have been a professional lover, and if she had been, the more likely designation would have been courtesan. Her iconography is of a pretty young woman being led by her dog, who tugs her along by a fold of her skirt held in his mouth towards the discovery of what is either the corpse of her lover or a more generalized *memento mori* in the form of a skeleton, presumably the incident that led to the reform of her life. Most female saints are classified as virgins, martyrs, widows and sometimes even queens. Obviously belonging to none of these designations, Margaret is venerated as a penitent, a truly honorable kind of saint when you consider that it is also the title given Mary Magdalen.

unknown. Some think they may have come from Asia Minor. A prime example of their art in the Academy in Cortona is a circular chandelier of sixteen oil-burning lamps ringed with bacchantes pursued by lascivious fauns. It was turned up by a farmer's plow not very long ago. The remnants of the Etruscans are everywhere in Cortona.

Streets of Cortona
circa 1991

Beyond the artistic and historic attractions of the town, Cortona is just a very nice place to be. The younger kids kicking a soccer ball around the piazza were a sort of counterpoint to the teenage girls strolling arm-linked in twos and threes, happy to be admired by the young men who stood on the corners watching the girls. The extreme climb and descent necessary for getting about the town have produced a crop of younger women with very good legs and older ones who would appear to have a touch of arthritis from the dogged, inevitable way they climb the steep streets. But people of all ages in Cortona seem to take appropriate enjoyment from being who they are, at any age.

The town is interested in things like the price of beef cattle on the hoof, the quality of this year's olive oil harvest, and the length of the season for maturing the grapes from the acres of vineyards that mantle the neighboring hills about the town. The colors of the countryside are deep ruddy brown of Umbrian soil and the silver-green of the olive trees that are everywhere about.

We found one restaurant that had good food but an overly pretentious way about it. On our second night we located the Trattoria Grotta where the host was gracious and enthusiastic, the *vitella piccate* pounded to the thinness of lily petals, and the new season's asparagus an adventure still unforgotten. The town is well known for its good food and is the only place I have ever heard of that celebrates the feast of the Assumption of Mary (August 15) with a Beefsteak Festival. Cortona has long been a refuge for artists and writers, from Boston's Henry James to North Carolina's Virginia Wright-Frierson. It is off the main roads and has no railroad station, but its lofty mountaintop is bounded by spectacular views of Umbria and Tuscany from every window.

XVII.

SIENA

A Happy Look Backward to the Sorrows
of the Middle Age

W E CAME TO Siena from the north by car through southern Tuscany and toured the rolling countryside for several
hours. The April landscape was green with silvery olive
trees and rich red, newly ploughed soil. Each hill was
topped with a tuft of woods, a single tree, a stone barn
and farmhouse, or occasionally an entire village. In one
of the villages we stopped at the only *Alimentari* and negotiated with a pair of rotund, delightfully friendly ladies
for a hero sandwich of noble proportions. It was assembled
with great care, replete with *pecorino, pomodoro, prosciutto,*
salami, and various assorted vegetables well sprinkled with
good olive oil. Sectioned with the Swiss army knife[1] and
accompanied by a bottle of local white wine, it might

---

[1] Always have one in your pocket or your shoulder bag when travelling.

have provided provender for a family for several days had
we not dispatched the whole thing in a leisurely picnic
along the roadside. I cannot recall the name of the wine
but it came off the shelf of the store, cost about $1.35 and
was just right with that monumental sandwich.

Following the necessary nap in the car, we pressed
on to the west and were eventually rewarded by the sight,
uphill from us, of the wonderful silhouette of Siena's
Duomo against a pale orange sky. Like most of the cathe-
drals in Italy, the building is huge. Giovanni Pisano started
designing it in the older, Romanesque style. (His father,
Nicola Pisano sculpted the wonderful pulpit.) They
worked upward in a layercake of black and white marble
bands, building the bicolored columns that look like stacks
of checkers, rearing arches and massive buttresses. They
eventually finished it with a wonderful dome designed
by yet another architect. But before they were done, in
the height of the town's prosperity, the powers that were
decided to make their cathedral the greatest in the world.
This Tower of Babel kind of town planning was gener-
ated by an abundance of economic success and overreach-
ing civic pride. Neither the Roman gods nor the
Christian deity are very forgiving of this sort of project
management. Almost predictably, they lost their next war
with Florence, an ongoing Guelph versus Ghibelline soccer match that was tied 2-2 in the third quarter at the
time. This is what comes of sticking the municipal neck
out too far. They had started building the new cathedral
by using what is now the nave as crossing and transepts
for the enormous structure. The towering arches that were

to form the north wall of the great new nave were built as was most of the west facade. These segments outline what the building was intended to encompass when the great plan was complete. But the setback by Florence turned out to be a relatively permanent condition when the black death visited Siena three times in the mid-fourteenth century and almost depopulated the town.[2] The church was finished as we see it today, and pretty fine at that. Although the gargantuan scale of the project was abandoned never to be resumed, you can climb a spiral stair inside that free-standing north wall and look out from the parapet on what would have been the line of the eaves above the clerestory. It's an impressive conception.

Siena is colorful in many ways. To begin with, the pigments raw and burnt sienna are made from clays of the local soil whence they are exported around the world. Raw sienna is a nice gutsy, brownish yellow; the cooked variety is a rich, ruddy orange brown that finds a place on virtually every artist's palette. It is also the basic color of

---

[2] We have all heard of this plague but most of us know little about it. It may have been bubonic carried by rat fleas but it might also have been anthrax brought to Europe by shipments of Asian horses. In either case it was swift and deadly. Swellings in the armpits and groin were followed by spitting up blood. Death came in about three days. I don't know how many died in Siena, but the population of Florence dropped from one hundred thousand to less than fifty thousand in the years between 1348 and 1351. Parts of Europe were largely depopulated and something like thirty percent of the population died in the late fourteenth century. No one knew what caused it or what could stop it, although burning witches, self-flagellation, and the murder of Jews were variously tried as remedies.

all the roof tiles, stucco, and brick in Italy, except in neighboring Umbria where they are, naturally, a little more
umber-colored.

But the more exciting accent colors in Siena are the
flags of the seventeen *contrade*, the neighborhood divi-
sions of the town that rival each other in the fierce parti-
sanship of their residents. Each neighborhood has a symbol on its banner, delineated in bright primary hues of
the full color spectrum. The symbols are an eagle, a snail,
a dolphin, a rhinoceros, a turtle and porcupine. There are
also the owl, the unicorn, a scallop, elephant, caterpillar,
dragon, giraffe, goat, panther, wolf and a duck. Most of
the beasts wear crowns, or bear banners in their pictures
which adorn the flags you see everywhere. The elephant
has a castle on his back and the eagle has two heads. They
are a very agreeable menagerie, and I debated buying a
set of the flags for some paltry sum at a rather nice tourist
stand near the Campo. But what I thought of at the time
as better judgment overcame the urge, and having returned home I have ever since regretted my mistaken stin-
giness. I may someday make a pilgrimage back to Siena
just to acquire a set of those wonderful gonfalons. They
would look superb as "dressing ship" flags on my little
boat on the Connecticut River on the Fourth of July or
Labor Day.

The Campo is the scallop-shell-shaped heart of Siena,
rimmed by shops and cafés and closed off on the more or
less straight northeastern side by the slightly concave facade of the Palazzo Pubblico. On the second floor of this
building is the municipal art gallery, which houses won-

derful paintings allegorizing good and bad government to the edification of the city council in whose chambers they decorate the walls. It has a bell tower called the Torre del Mangia, a designation which probably has to do with eating but does nothing to detract from its grace and extreme height. The top half-dozen stories of the structure are made of white travertine stone which makes a wonderful contrast with the slim brick shaft. The color scheme reminds me of the white painted topmasts above the oiled pine spars of the old fishing schooners.[3]

But likening the tower to a mast is hardly appropriate to the scale of the thing; the Torre is 102 meters tall, in the same league with the much earlier Cremona and Modenese spires, and taller than a thirty-story building. Even in this era of steel framing and stressed-skin architecture, a tower of more than 330 feet is impressive. Considering it was made of mortared masonry in a land noted for its earthquakes, it seems almost miraculous that it should be here at all 650 years after it was built as an offering to God for remitting the plagues of the black death. Somehow, in spite of its grand scale, it is clearly less an act of hubris than the planned enlargement of the cathedral. We settled into white plastic chairs at a table of

---

[3] There are replicas of the Italian towers in many parts of the world. My favorite is in Waterbury, Connecticut, where a half-scale tower rises gracefully above the railroad station, a symbol of civic pride that matched the attitude of the Sienese of the late Middle Ages. It bespeaks confidence in a prosperous future and the permanence of worldly success, in this case of the New York, New Haven and Hartford Railroad which went bankrupt in the 1960s.

an outdoor café on the upper rim of the Campo and watched the tower march through the cloud-flecked blue sky in a nice breeze.

Siena Palazzo Publico
1288-1309

Our hotel, the Chiusarelli, was a touch down at the heels, but quite clean, comfortable, and at that time less than L100,000 for the night. It is located on the busy Viale Curtatone which runs along a ridge separating the deep lowland that contains Saint Catherine's house from another valley that is the site of the Communal Soccer

Stadium. Many Italian towns are built on a series of hills, but Siena seems to have been settled on escarpments, gorges, cliffs, ravines, and quarry pits in middle-sized mountains. If you plot your course carefully, you can get around town on the ridges without too much climbing. But if you take a straight shot from the great church of St. Dominic to the Campo, you will go down and up the equivalent of five or six stories. Our room at the Chiusarelli looked down on the soccer stadium. Had there been a game, we could have sold seats in our bedroom.

The two midsummer horse races around the Campo for the *il Palio* are extolled in all the touristic literature about Siena. They are said to be a great show each time, but they also jam the city with other tourists and take place in the expensive high season. We've not been. Maybe someday.

The art in Siena, both the late medieval Sienese school and the early Renaissance work, is hard to summarize and impossible to catalogue here. The cathedral and baptistry together probably contain the best collection, but there is a lot to be seen. This building is replete with works of Pisano, Ghiberti, and Jacopo della Quercia. Upstairs is the Duomo proper where the *pavimento* was inlaid with biblical scenes by the best artists, a swatch at a time for over two hundred years until 56 areas were delineated in the floor. Pisano's wonderful pulpit is also here, showing Romulus and Remus being suckled by their adoptive mother, the she-wolf, under the preacher's feet. The building provides enough material for a good course in art history. Thanks offerings to various protecting saints are particularly interesting, whether commemorating being rid of the Nazis in the mid-twentieth century or being spared the wrath of the Florentines in the mid-thirteenth, about equally grisly alternatives to the Sienese of those times. We allowed the greater part of a day for the cathedral, with time out for a good lunch. Even so we didn't see it all. We resolved to come back again another day to soak in the beauty of this medieval town.

The Renaissance never really got to Siena. The city went straight from the gothic to a few adventures with the later baroque. The Sienese passed the greatest part of the fifteenth and sixteenth centuries under the scourge of the plague, the heel of Florence, the domination of the Spanish Hapsburg Emperor Charles V, or the elegant iron fist of the Medici. One result has been the preservation of the medieval city, unaltered by Renaissance prosperity, today smiling, sweet and finally prosperous again.

XVIII.

THE BOYS OF THE RENAISSANCE
Clearly Related to Those of Today

ONCE, WHILE leafing through the glossy pages of a guidebook cataloging most of the contents of the Uffizi, it struck me with some surprise that the lavish exploration of human circumstance I was looking at was biased by both sex and age. There were many beautiful women of various stages of maturity, lots of babies and toddlers and a number of children. There were old men and gods in the form of patriarchs, mature men as warriors, dukes and knights. There are naked boys in the form of cupids and putti who are fat little blobs of masculinity flying around Tiepolo's ceilings. But there are relatively few older boys, young fellows in the physical flowering of their late teens or early twenties. Caravaggio painted early teenagers, at least one of whom he obviously liked, but Adam appears to have been created by God as a post-adolescent man of some maturity. He usually looks to be in his mid to early thirties as represented by most Renaissance artists.

Only a few, Titian, Pontormo, and his disciple Bronzino in particular, lavished much of their talent and attention on depictions of the immediately post-pubescent male. Bronzino's models are as much with us today in modern Italy as are the descendants of the girls who posed for Bellini and Raphael. (Finding a real Giorgione walking with her boyfriend in Milan or Rome is much rarer.) Pontormo's *Halberdier* is a good example of the

PONTORMO - Halberdier -1527

type rarely depicted by others: the painting abounds in phallic symbols of sword pommel and staff, although no halberd is evident. The young man's glance reveals an interior chemistry composed of about equal parts of testosterone and narcissism.

Pontormo's paintings emphasize the gallant, daring, self-admiration of the nineteen year old. Bronzino's youths are more intensely in need of relief, and look meltingly in the direction of the nearest female who might be persuaded to help them attain it. Both are in an obviously perpetual state of readiness for copulation for most of their waking (or sleeping) hours. The only surcease for this continuing state of rigidity would seem to be in relatively brief post-coital intervals. Their lives are thus a continuing quest for consummation wherever it might be found.

Titian's *Young Man in the Red Cap* is now in New York at the Frick Collection. But his double, with the same deep brown, painfully passion-filled eyes, sits at the little tables in café bars, in Venice or Verona, reaching across the table to hold both of the hands of some ravishing teenaged beauty that he contemplates with wordless desire. The melting gaze has a sort of 750 watt microwave quality that will surely turn the young lady's heart and resolution to the viscosity of a *crema caramella* after a few minutes exposure.

I saw a perfect modern example of Pontormo's young man-at-arms strolling the Milanese galleria with his companion, one arm circling her waist, his hand lodged in the far side rear hip pocket of her tight blue jeans, where it was securely held in a permanent and possessive caress of her buttocks. His imperious stare at the rest of the world reflected great pride in the acquisition of the franchise he thus displayed.

Sculpture of young men is another matter. Oddly, the nude male is far more chaste than the clothed models of the paintings. The dreamy gaze of Michelangelo's *David* has nothing of desire in it. The various Apollos are all quite apollonian, and Mercury, flashy and speedy as he may be, is bent on obediently delivering the messages of the gods rather than his own *billets-doux*.

Perhaps the sexless quality of the male nudes of the Renaissance comes from the association of all other young male nakedness with the two most often depicted during the period: the deposition of the dead Christ and the arrow-riddled body of the standing Saint Sebastian. Those flaccid bodies are archetypes of Italian art. Any hint of the turgid sexuality of the real young male is close to sacrilege. If the eyes of the model are to convey any suggestion of that perpetually burning, tormented search for a companion in detumescence, the body must be covered up by the luxurious raiment of the young courtier or soldier. In any case it must be unmistakably removed from any similarity to the stripped bodies of Sebastian or Jesus.

Even aside from outright sexuality, affection among contemporary Italian males is displayed differently from the way Americans are used to. Once at lunch in a pizzeria in a small Italian town we vicariously enjoyed a birthday party for a young man in his twenties. There was much laughter and teasing over the glasses of wine and whipped-cream covered desserts. The birthday boy then made a short speech and thanked all of the guests by making the full circuit of the table kissing every one on both cheeks, men and women alike. Watching high school students setting off to class reveal a similar ease with physical affection that American kids could never emulate. As the time to enter the building approached, the whole group said farewell for the next few hours with many hugs and kisses on both cheeks, boys with girls, girls with girls, and boys with boys. It also occurred to me that young American males would be horrified to be seen in public with the book-filled back packs that their Italian counterparts strapped on. The design of the rucksacks was the same but the boys in Italy favored bags made of pink, lavender, and spring green nylon canvas.

XIX.

FLORENCE
The Full Bloom of the Renaissance with the Motorini *at Full Bore*

DESPITE THE confusing series of impressions Firenze made on us when we first arrived, the meaning of it all became clear when we considered the source of the startling contrasts. It is a city of beauty and dirt, a jarring juxtaposition of powerful ancient architecture and roaring modern motor vehicles, a place of Tuscan sunshine and Los Angeles smog. For Florence is about money and it always has been. Money both produced and now defiles its beauty.

One of the town's earliest great municipal boasts is that this little city, which is even today only little more than the size of Bridgeport, Connecticut, undertook seven hundred years ago to build the largest cathedral in the world. They named it for Saint Mary of the Flowers and constructed the greatest part of it in less than twenty years, although it took over another century to close in its crossing with the largest dome attempted since the Romans roofed the Pantheon. No vengeful deity struck them down for their pride. They financed the project not on the resources of a continental empire, but from the money they made in wool, dyeing and leather. They only lost the dome-span-and-altitude title several hundred years later when the popes built St.Peter's by tapping the wealth of all of North Europe from the sale of indulgences to those in terror of the punishment due to their manifest sinfulness. And, of course, although Rome seems an appropriate place for such a wonder, the popes were chastised for their ambition a few years after their dome was built by the outbreak of the Reformation.

But Rome is about power, whereas Florence is about money, and money can buy great art if the artists are given their freedom, while power cannot command art to serve it. Artists are notorious for subverting the power of absolute rulers, temporal as well as spiritual. I think this is why some Roman religious art looks theologically rebellious, even cynical. Artists will work quite honestly for an honest wage, but not at the absolute command of some ruler. This is why so much of the "Post Office Art" of the WPA is quite wonderful, while the contemporaneous mural production of the Soviet Union is so dreadful.

The immense dome of the Florentine cathedral was not designed by the original architect of the church, Arnolfo di Cambio. He died only six years into the project and left not a scrap of design for spanning the dome. Work went on for a long time while the great octagonal drum that crowned the crossing was left roofless for want of a plan to span it.

When the youthful Filippo Brunelleschi had come in second in the famous competition for the bronze doors of the Florentine baptistry,[1] he travelled to Rome with his friend Donatello and saw for the first time the remains of the classical architecture of Rome. Only a few intact Roman buildings were left, but then as now, the domed Pantheon was one of them. It is hard for us to realize, in our age of swift travel and photography, how amazing the first view of a city only a few hundred kilometers away from home could be. Brunelleschi, who was also a skilled engineer, was staggered by what he found and set to work to measure the ruins and to draw plans of what the ancient buildings must have been like. Later, when he returned to Florence, he offered to design the dome for Santa Maria del Fiore, but because he was still in his twenties, he suggested that architects from all over Europe be asked to compete for the job. It took a number of years for the guild masters to decide that he should have the commission unencumbered by the ideas of other designers. He insisted that he could construct the dome without a center scaffold to hold it up while under construction, although he didn't tell in advance how he would accomplish this feat. (Sky hooks?) The clear span of the opening was 132 feet[2] and the windowed lantern at the

---

[1] Lorenzo Ghiberti won the contest, evidently on the recommendation of Donatello and Brunelleschi himself. The trial panels and the winner's strongly three dimensional reliefs can be seen just across the piazza from the cathedral.

[2] It could contain a baseball diamond with room for first and third base coaches' boxes.

top was designed to stand over 300 feet above the floor below. At the time it was to be the tallest building in Italy. Brunelleschi's plan required the construction of a pair of concentric, octagonal ribbed domes built of specially cast interlocking bricks that hooked each to each and held themselves together as the work progressed from the outer rim up to the center. As the heavy material piled up above, chains embedded in the masonry kept the bottom from spreading. The finished design we see today is entirely dictated by the functional requirements of getting it built. It is about as free of extraneous decoration as John Roebling's Brooklyn Bridge. The space between the shells is large enough to contain kitchens for preparing the masons' dinner at midday. In later years, Michelangelo and Christopher Wren designed spans a few feet larger for St. Peter's and St. Paul's. Both acknowledged their debt to Brunelleschi's daring engineering. Michelangelo said his design was the sister of the Florentine model, perhaps a little bigger but not more beautiful than the dome of Santa Maria del Fiore.

Older than the cathedral's dome is the Campanile or bell tower. It was designed by Giotto around 1334 when the construction began, and was finished a half century after his death. Reliefs by Andrea Pisano and Luca della Robbia were added as the work went along, but the design of the vertical lines and panels is very much the work of the old master who created the chapel in Padua and the frescoes in the lower chapel at Assisi. It might seem odd to us that a painter such as Giotto should be a brilliant architect too, but that was really the case of all the

tered, continues unabated, giving an ironic twist to the nursery rhyme that kept coming around in my head.

> Giro, girotondo
> Come è bell' il mondo![4]

Although I really try to keep the image of the lavish distribution of internal combustion engines from dominating my memory of Florence, I think that oft-repeated walk into the oldest part of town scarred my sensibility. The peace of central Ferrara and the almost eerie silence of Venice come to mind as alternatives to the noisy pursuit of gain that propels the never-ending flow of cars, Vespas and motorcycles around and around the baptistry, campanile and cathedral. I cannot imagine that a huge amount of profit would be foregone if a year-round traffic-free zone were proclaimed in the downtown.

Florence is, like Rome, impossible to catalog without a whole book devoted to it. Thanks mostly to the Medici, it houses the greatest collections of art in the world, and being in Florence, the Florentines charge the most for viewings: L10,000 for the Uffizi, and slightly less for the other museums. It's not that they're not worth it; they surely are. But by the time you have spent a full day among three or four, several of which are not large, it is easy to drop well over $20 just getting in and out of the galleries. It discourages repeat visits and drop-ins. But never

---

[4]Roughly translated, and to the tune of:
Ring around the rosie
How the world is lovely!

mind, eat the best food in Modena and Bologna where the museums are cheap and dine simply in Florence where Botticelli reigns supreme.

Sandro Botticelli is surely one of the reasons to come to Italy in the first place.[5] From among many great paintings, there are two absolutely stupendous nudes in the Uffizi, Titian's *Venus of Urbino*, and Botticelli's *Birth of Venus*. The former would cause an uproar among the political and religious right if it were shown on early evening television in the United States. The latter presents an equally naked mythological beauty so pure that she could be exhibited in the refectory of a seminary. Less than sixty years of time separates these two beautiful women, but an ocean of differentiated taste and sensibility lies between.

The most famous and often-reproduced lady on the shell[6] is only one of Botticelli's paintings here. I grew up in a house where a good, large-scale print of the *Madonna of the Magnificat* hung in a circular frame in the living room. Finally seeing the real thing, full-sized about

---

[5] He was on the Medici payroll for most of his life and gave full measure for their patronage. Almost thirty of his paintings are in the gallery that used to be their "office" building, the Uffizi. If one could rank a few of them as less successful than others, it could only be in comparison to the exaltation of his most wonderful works. Any one of his paintings would qualify as the capolavoro of nearly any other painter.

[6] And she was indeed a lady—sort of. She was Simonetta Catteneo, the wife of Marco Vespucci, brother of the well-travelled Amerigo, for whom our country is named. Simonetta was also the beloved of Giuliano de' Medici, who paid Botticelli's salary. Giuliano also shows up as Mercury in the springtime painting, and with his brother as an attendant angel in the round *Madonna of the Magnificat*.

twice the dimension of the childhood memory, was an exciting moment. And then, of course, there is the companion piece to Venus, *la Primavera*.

It would be fruitless to try to compile even a small list of the masterworks commissioned and collected by the Florentines. Michelangelo was, of course, a Florentine. His huge *David* with its oddly disproportionate hands is a staggering thing to see. For most of us it is a surprise that it is as big as it is, perhaps also surprising is that Michelangelo left his youthful Jewish hero uncircumcised. I guess his idea of young male perfection was more a Greek or Roman archetype than a historical recreation. We discovered that the real *David* is in the Accademia; the one in the Piazza della Signoria is a copy made in the nineteenth century when it was decided to get the original in out of the rain. It was a wise decision; the mixture of soot and automobile exhaust has played hob with most of the exposed marble in Florence.

We had made some preparation for visiting Florence by reading Vasari's *Lives of the Artists* years before, but we could have done a lot more research to our profit. Vasari's accounts are brief, but they give a feeling for the life in Renaissance Florence. Of course, it takes more than one trip to get to know it. Seeing the whole richness of the Florentine art collections at one time was more than I could handle. You must see a bit and then learn something about it if you are to come away with anything but a sensation of surfeit from the experience.

The museums and galleries in Florence contain a great wealth of oil and tempera paintings, not all of them Italian. Cranach and Dürer are well-represented. Their

Adam and Eves show how differently north and south
European artists saw ideal form. But however potbellied
and awkward their Eves, the northerners win out with
their portraits. Holbein's painting of Sir Richard Southwell
is my candidate for the finest portrait in the Uffizi. Hans
Memling's Virgins, in spite of having a faint resemblance
to Popeye's girl friend Olive Oyle, are exquisitely painted
and teeming with natural details from the increasingly
prosperous quality of life in Renaissance Germany.

And then are the great frescoes of Florence. But you
must do the rounds of the churches to see them.
Pontormo's *Virgin of the Annunciation* was done with the
assistance of his young apprentice, Bronzino. Mary is
startled, submissive, curious, and as lovely as the dawn in
that moment when she hears the news of her maternity
from the Angel. Gabriel almost seems to be averting his
beauty-blinded eyes as though he cannot bear to look
directly on the perfection of the Virgin. This 1528 fresco
is in the Capponi Chapel of the Chiesa Santa Felicità,
cleaned and remounted on its original wall with what a
guidebook called "the clumsy restorations of the eighteenth and nineteenth centuries" removed.[7]

---

[7] Restoration of works of art is a major industry in Italy. They have gotten
better at it over the years, and now they leave great gaps in damaged frescoes
rather than trying to repaint them to look as they originally did. One of
the rules is that whatever is added now must be removable when techniques
may have improved later on. The restorer's trade is an old one and has
given current usage to a common word in our language. Missing pieces of
marble statuary from Roman times were patched with sealing wax, tinted
so cleverly to match the stone that it took an eagle eye to notice it. Perfect
pieces of marble were labeled in Latin as *sin cerà*, "without wax," from
which we get our word "sincere."

There is, of course, an Annunciation in virtually every church in Florence, many of them magnificent. I haven't seen half of them.

We did, however, spend a leisurely morning in the Piazza della Signoria, and its accompanying loggia, where the world's greatest collection of statues seems to stand around rather casually just because that is where they happen to be this morning. We went on to see the Bargello, the doors of the baptistry, and the contents of that ninth century building itself.

The fact is that there is altogether too much art in Florence. It is impossible for a tourist to get around in a way that will allow its appreciation. You simply have to go at it a little bit at a time and come back several more times. Otherwise you will experience that sensory overload that many critics and travellers have commented on in the past, and, in the process, miss seeing a great deal of what you are looking at. My senses were so glutted with Donatello, Verocchio, Michelangelo, Raffaello, Veronese, Correggio, and Leonardo and all the others that I can't recall a single restaurant we ate in the first three nights we spent in the city. And we never even got inside the Pitti Palace or the great portrait gallery in Vasari's *corridoro* that runs across the top of the Ponte Vecchio and connects the palace with the Uffizi.

Feeling a little inebriated by it all we decided it was time to head south to a more manageable venue.

XX.

ORVIETO
Atop the Stump of an Old Volcano,
Surrounded by Grapes

SOUTH OF TUSCANY and Umbria on the way to Rome, we first saw Orvieto as a jagged group of houses and a few towers crowning a massive plug of volcanic rock. The sides of the mountain are impressive cliffs that inspired the Etruscans to make it a stronghold almost three thousand years ago. Even though some of their language can be read today by clever scholars, we still know very little about them. The Romans almost totally obliterated their civilization by making it illegal to speak or write their language. This form of cultural genocide could be remarkably effective in the years before the printing press. Manuscripts were few and inscriptions on monuments terse and uninformative. The Etruscans learned to speak Latin in a generation or so, and their language simply disappeared. Their descendants became Roman in both culture and citizenship. But wherever the hill towns of north-central Italy present their fantastic silhouettes to the sky, you will find evidence that the Etruscans were there first. Huge, roughly shaped stone walls at the very crests of nearly unclimbable heights signal that they settled here eight centuries before the Caesars. I wonder if they had an heroic poetry of their own, full of wars, and blood and honor. Or were their forbidding strongholds little courts of safety where love songs were sung and amorous youths and maidens dallied in the warm climate of Latium? That great circular chandelier in Cortona is decorated with figures that surely exalt human desire, whether only of satyrs, bacchantes or other dancers I cannot be sure. Will we ever be able to read the Etruscans' songs? Did they sing?

The train stops below the town in the flat valley of the immature Tiber. Busses and taxis scale the crag and eventually deposit tourists in the Piazza del Duomo. Pope Clement VII waited out the horrible sack of Rome here in the early sixteenth century when the various ungoverned mercenary troops of the Emperor Charles V had their savage way with the imperial city. The square in Orvieto is peaceful and hardly seems large enough to support the immense facade of the cathedral that completely dominates the city. It is a stretch to call it a city, composed of less than 25,000 inhabitants on the rock above the plain, the town is less than half the size of Wilmington, North Carolina. I don't know how much smaller it may have been during the early thirteenth century when they raised that lofty pile. It may have been larger then. The changing fortunes of war and plague over the centuries make it hard to say for sure.

On either side of the doors of the cathedral are a series of bas-reliefs that display the same teaching about the creation of man, and his *peccato originale*, and the final judgment of the blessed and the damned that was usually depicted on church portals in the Middle Ages and the early Renaissance. The guidebooks are a little vague about who made them and when, but the likely candidate is Lorenzo Maitani, the architect who completed the cathedral and gave the facade its colorful triple gables. He also did much of the interior before his death in 1330. The reliefs are wonderful, delicately modeled, and presage the work of della Quercia in Bologna.

On the left is a most human pair of first parents. A robed God the Father removing Eve from Adam's side with surgical precision, and a pair of vengeful angels hustling the couple out of paradise. Then an oppressed Adam wields a mattock while his still naked lady looks the other way, sitting like Miss Muffit on a tuffet and spinning flax by hand. Almost all of the important scenes of both Old and New Testaments are there, flanking the central portal. On the far right pier there is an orderly tangle of figures showing the resurrection of the dead, their judgment, the ascent of the blessed and the just desserts coming to those who have failed in this life at the bottom. The panels are separated and connected by twining ivies that seem espaliered on the marble blocks of the pilasters. I have seen nothing like it anywhere else in Europe. These scriptural stories in stone are crowned by huge fantastic bronzes of the emblems of the evangelists: the angel, the lion, the eagle and the bull. The whole effect is appropriately apocalyptic. For more than six centuries the faithful have been contemplating the beginnings and ends of important things as they pass through those portals. The effect of the whole facade is to put one's own prayer for the petty ups and downs of daily life in a proper perspective. Inside the cathedral the same themes of death, damnation, resurrection and salvation are displayed in the frescoes of Luca Signorelli. Begun at the very end of the quatrocento they are often cited as among the earliest of the sort of compositions of the crowds of nude figures that became the stock in trade of the mannerist painters in the next century. The Orvieto frescoes of Signorelli are thought to have had a profound influence on the young Michelangelo, who undoubtedly saw and examined them. Today, they have a certain naive quality compared to Michelangelo's work, but they are stunning. While all the medieval and Renaissance artists were quite proficient at conveying the horrors of hell, Signorelli is at the top of the list in showing us the resurrection and the approach to beatitude. His reassembled bodies are coming out of the grave like summer bathers who had been buried for a nap on the beach. They lift themselves from the sands in which they have spent but an afternoon awaiting their release to eternity. They are nearly naked, their loins simply looped with colored scarves of striped Roman silk. Their hair is long, mostly blond and their bodies are those of late teenagers. Their expressions are wide-eyed with innocent curiosity. While archangelic trumpeters summon them from above with six-foot instruments, other angels play mandolins and guitars to acccompany their rising. There is a blythe Woodstock quality to the whole scene.

Perhaps the daily contact with so much great religious art accounts for the virtues of many Italians. The institutional church seems to have little effect on most of them. Their sex lives are untrammeled, their abortions as frequent and their disrespect for chatechetical rules are as flagrant as any people in Europe. Yet they act like St. Francis when they can and will usually do the Christian thing when their good will is called for. Since the preachers don't seem to be the source of such behavior, I think it may come from the art.

While in Orvieto, we sampled their famous wine *in situ*. Ours was a brief stop and I do feel it would be worthwhile to come back and pass more time here. There are many sights to see and several good hotels and guest houses in town, as well as any number of restaurants. The pace of life seems less heroic here than in the larger cities. I guess that's why the popes used it as a getaway in times of trouble.

XXI.

ROME
A Very Brief Mention of the Eternal City

Rome is not like the rest of Italy. There is too much art, too much religion, too great an Empire, and more than 260 popes. It is a city not of a people, but of one man: the latest emperor, dictator, or the current successor of the fisherman. And for every statement that might be made about them there are dozens of exceptions. Even the *Catholic Encyclopedia Dictionary* suffixes a disclaimer to its assertion that Pius XI was number 261 as "the most reliable number." That would make John Paul, the first Polish pope, number 266 in the line since Peter. But there are also a score or more of antipopes, most of whom reigned in France and some of them were quite as holy as those who were designated as real popes by the subsequent papacies. The whole collection includes the saintly, the scholarly, the legalistic, the bloody-minded, the ecstatic, the mercenary, the military, the political, the visionary, the punitive, the ignorant and the wise in generous measure.

Many had huge chunks of the great architecture of the city they took over pulled down to reuse its stone for their own projects. Others have collected and safeguarded the art of past ages and commissioned some of the greatest achievements of human imagination. Still others have forbade the teaching of truth for fear it might upset faith. Only a few have taken refuge in the "Doctrine of Infallibility" and those (since Pius IX) really recognized that its proclamation at the first Vatican Council was largely a piece of nineteenth-century theological bravado in the face of the loss of political and military power. Almost all in recent times have been celibate in behavior as well as theory, although Peter was not. But some have had full and abundantly fruitful relationships with women, while others feared women and felt that sexual congress was almost always sinful (even though necessary for the "continuation of the species"). At the very least, modern popes and their doctrinal advisors consider the sexual desire of men and women for each other to be a fundamental source of sin, and among the worst things that can distract mankind from the primacy of another, better world.

Only a few recent popes, such as Pius XII and Paul VI, were intellectuals. John XXIII, whose simplicity of manner masked his commanding intelligence, lived close enough for us to really know him. He was a plain man of great faith who spoke of docility to the promptings of the Holy Spirit and seems to have loved all men, women, children, criminals, sexual deviants, communists, Jews, Moslems, Protestants, peasants, business men, babies and politicians.

Despite its history, there seems to be little in the capital city of the old Empire that has much of anything to do with the Carpenter's Son of Nazareth, the Historical Jesus, the Mythic Christ, or the Word of the Gospel of John. Even if you are an American Christian, Catholic, Episcopalian or denominational Protestant, Rome may or may not reinforce the state of mind you come with. Direct contact with Rome has turned some Catholics into cynical non-believers just as it has often confirmed the faith of other pilgrims. The almost magical environments created by Bramante, Michelangelo, Raphael, and Bernini have forced more than a few Anglicans to their knees in a flood of believing tears, not just a response to a sort of theological stage setting, but a recognition of the power of the faith that moved the artists to such titanic achievements. The visible faith of the far-flung church is inspirational; the vast wealth of the papacy is a scandal to many. Rome is not a city to be taken lightly.

Bernini is surely the artist of papal Rome, while Michelangelo speaks for all the world. As we can see it today, the Basilica of Saint Peter is Bernini's work. Michelangelo's dome is nearly invisible from the Bernini Piazza around the obelisk and his frescos in the Sistine Chapel are not visible to Romans at all, only to tourists who spend a few minutes viewing them as they speed along their tour. But Bernini's serpentine columns supporting the *baldacchino* are there for all to see in the church as well as in the newspaper photographs of the pope saying his prayers. Bernini's enormous sunburst, which is the focus of attention at the far end of the huge apse, is the ultimate baroque icon glorifying the Chair of Peter, the symbol of the power of the Papacy. This center of theological and political force is made explicit by the explosion of baroque putti who radiate from the dove of the Holy Spirit that floats over the pope's empty chair, that rises even higher than the very altar where he celebrates Mass. Nowhere else is it more clear that Rome is about power.

Bernini, who lived in the baroque fullness of the seventeenth century,[1] was the most brilliant sculptor of his age as well as the most Roman. He modeled himself as a damned soul and carved the result in marble. Bernini's head and shoulders show anger, force, perhaps even insanity, but the expression lacks the abysmal hopelessness of Michaelangelo's despairing soul staring out from the Last Judgement, clearly caught in the final stupefying knowledge of his sure and irretrievable damnation for all ages to come.

Perhaps one should not go to Rome on a first trip to Italy. It is essentially a different culture from the North, and it could be better assimilated after gaining some skill in negotiating the country and the language. Learn your way around Renaissance art first. For Rome was a back-

---

[1]He was a contemporary of John Milton and about thirty years older than Galileo. Spiritually and intellectually, he seems much closer to the latter than the former.

BERNINI as a Damned Soul
c.1619

water and the pope in France at Avignon during most of
the years when the great artists shaped the new sensibility
in the fourteenth century. Later, in the quattrocento, even
strong popes like Martin V Colonna fled the city for years
at a time and lived in Florence. Thus the artistic history of
Rome largely skips from the classical period of the empire to the late Renaissance, mannerist, and baroque periods. Rome was nearly deserted during the Romanesque
and the Gothic ages. The popes missed the cool purity of
Piero della Francesca, the delicate simplicity of the Bellinis,

and the disciplined inventiveness of Mantegna. Only later, with Raphael and Michelangelo, did Rome come into its own. Even then, Rome is a city consisting of architecture rather than painting. During the baroque age of Caravaggio and the later painters, connoisseur popes begin to collect European art for their palaces in the Vatican. It is wonderful to see, but all this became more visible to us only after we had first explored extensively in northern Italy. After all, a first trip to Italy implies a preface to a second trip.

Still, lunching at a sidewalk café in the Piazza Navona and enjoying the waterfalls of Bernini's Fountain of the Four Rivers is a pleasant way to pass an afternoon. We may also have been unwitting extras in one of the movies that seem to use this relic of the Emperor Domitian's old stadium as a backdrop on an almost daily basis.

XXII.

MILAN
To the Cultural Capital and Home

WE HAVE STARTED most of our Italian voyages in Milan. As our trips came to an end, we returned. We had already negotiated the subway, *la metropolitana*, and were considerably less intimidated by the big city the second time. And Milan is a big city. The train travelled through seemingly endless suburbs, we looked over a great number of backyards and walled gardens, and finally rose on a sort of elevated mole that gave us a panorama of a large, modern, slightly grubby cityscape. The Stazione Centrale F.S. is one of those vast Victorian sheds of semicircular riveted iron arches that spans a dozen or more tracks, open on the outboard end, and, full of the exciting sounds and smells of railroad trains. The metal arches rise nearly a hundred feet overhead. It must have been even more exciting when the station was also filled with clouds of steam and antique engines puffing columns of smoke. We dismounted and looked for a baggage trolley, and finding none, we learned then and there that the airline crews' wheeled cases with integral pull-out handles are essential for senior travellers. From where we left the train to the inside of the terminal, along the asphalt platform beside the tracks was about a third of a mile trek.

The Fielding guidebook's reliable recommendation aimed us toward the Gran Duca di York[1] symbolized by a suit of ersatz armor standing at the front door of the pleasant little hotel. We liked it but on another occasion found the Hotel Star on the Via Bossi, only three or four blocks from the opera house, La Scala. Once again, we had missed

---

[1] There have been many Dukes of York over the years, but the one the Italians love best was one of the Jacobite Pretenders, Henry, younger brother of Bonnie Prince Charlie who was himself Pretender to being Prince of Wales. After the dreadful defeat of his brother at Culloden, York was made a cardinal by the pope in the following year. Later he was ordained a priest and, eventually, a bishop. He outlived both the Old and Younger Pretenders, eventually becoming the last of the Stuart line. Ever ready to stick it in the ear of a Protestant English king, the pope had the old chevalier buried in a magnificent baroque sarcophagus in Saint Peter's, under the name "Jacobus III, Rex Angliorum," thus declaring the illegitimacy of the entire line of England's Hanoverian sovereigns. Although he had made the "rightful" next in line a cardinal, the pope did little to support him: Cardinal York lacked lands and benefices to furnish his state in proper Roman style. The Stuarts had fled England with little of value except their silverware. They had some property in France, but that went in the French Revolution. Eventually York swapped the royal plate to his distant cousin George III for a pension from the British Crown sufficient to keep him in decent estate in Rome until he died. He is buried beneath his father in St. Peter's, and the German sovereigns of Britannia have reigned pretty much unchallenged ever since.

the opera season by a week, but the Tokyo Quartet was playing a program of two of the great late Beethoven string quartets. Although it was a case of being hung for a lamb rather than a sheep, we resolved to experience the great auditorium with chamber music if we could not have *opera lirica*. All tickets are dear at La Scala, but the sure knowledge that one lives but once helped firm our resolution.

La Scala is a wonderful building, both for music and for history. Our seats were in the rearmost row of a third-tier box. Fortunately, the front seats were unoccupied and we were able to move to the front edge of the box and survey the entire house as well as the stage. The acoustics of the vast hall were perfect, even for the four small string instruments, and the audience was enthusiastic. The Milanese are famous for the generosity of their applause when the work is performed well, but also known for their cries of derision if the artist does not live up to their standard. It is said that dreadful things have happened to croaking bassos and superannuated sopranos. On the night we were there, the Milanese loved both the quartet and the composer.

During the intermission, we conducted ourselves in the grand manner befitting the location and acquired glasses of champagne at the third-tier lobby bar. We then discovered a series of interconnecting passageways and rooms leading to the opera museum, a wonderful attic of operatic junk blended with paintings of former divas and their tenors. There was a death mask of Verdi, an oil sketch of Toscanini, a cast of Chopin's hands (rather small and slightly crooked), as well as any number of fans, Carmen sashes, winged helmets, swords, pistols, and generous, low-cut gowns of bygone Violettas and the simpler dresses of the Mimis. While it is worth half the ticket price to browse through it, you can't get through all of it in one intermission. We resolved to be in Milan for an opera sooner or later.

Milan has a clutch of good museums, but the Pinacoteca di Brera contains the most amazing paintings. Piero della Francesca's serene, if somewhat static, Madonna and Child with Saints includes our old friend from Urbino, Duke Federico Montefeltro, (with the nick in his nose). Caravaggio and Raphael are present, as are Titian, Tintoretto, and the best of the Flemish painters. Perhaps the most striking to me was the foot-first view of the foreshortened *Dead Christ* that Mantegna painted in his later years.

Rich though Milan's museums may be, the city's most impressive works of art are the side-by-side wonders of the Duomo and the Galleria. Very much in the heart of the busy financial district, the cathedral is an enormous gingerbread wedding cake of late Gothic fancy. It was started in the fourteenth century and decorated with many more than two thousand statues which are perched on every buttress and pillar. The whole wasn't finished until nearly five-hundred years of creative stone cutting had been expended. A splendid piazza overlooks the front (the latest part), and an elevator goes to the roof, where an encircling series of walkways takes you over the sloping marble slabs of the nave to the very brink of the façade. It is a wonderful chance to look at the intricacies of Gothic stone work, and affords a splendid view of the city spread out around you.

Across the street to the north is one of the main entries to the famous Galleria, another poetic fancy that stretches building materials to their maximum to encompass the architect's conceit. In this case the materials are wrought iron and glass. Arches spring from the roof-tops of five-story buildings to enclose a half-dozen city blocks in a gigantic greenhouse reminiscent of the Crystal Palace. Built in the 1870s to celebrate their new king, this indoor-outdoor space is the prototype for all the shopping malls that now decorate or encumber so much of suburban America. They just did it better in Milan over a century ago. There are sidewalk cafés, bookstores, fashionable ladies shops, banks, jewelers and art galleries in great profusion. Many Milanese take their passegiata around the cathedral square in the late afternoon, but in rain or wind they crowd into the Galleria by the thousands, continuing the arm in arm stroll in a kind of flying

Galleria Vittorio Emanuele II · Milano o.1875

wedge formation that makes pedestrian navigation problematic.

We took refuge in one of the larger cafés and ordered our accustomed aperitivo. The rain showed no sign of letting up, so we later moved over to the restaurant side and ordered our early, pre-concert supper. Chance placed us next to a Japanese couple around our age.

They spoke English pretty well but were having trouble negotiating with the waiter. I plunged in and helped. The man turned out to be a retired automobile executive who had spent four years working in Dearborn, Michigan, back in the early 1960s. Obviously he learned there what not to do to judge by the inverse success rate of the cars from Japan and Michigan in subsequent years. Our conversation attracted the attention of an Englishman at an adjoining table. He wasn't getting satisfaction from his waiter on the subject of a discolored clam (*vongolo sciupato?*) in his pasta. It is amazing how far you can get on a dozen lessons from Madame LaZonga and a few hours listening to tape recordings in the family car.

The Japanese couple were much amused with the idea that we had come from America and were about to hear Japanese musicians performing German music in an Italian opera house. I countered that it was even more curious that the quartet (whose first fiddler is a British-born American of Armenian extraction) are the "resident quartet," at Yale, not an hour's drive from our home in Connecticut.

Like many of the north Italian cities, Milan came under the successive domination of powerful families and their descendants. The Visconti held it in thrall for most of the thirteenth through the fifteenth centuries. There was a short-lived Ambrosian republic around 1450, and then the Sforzas took over, smashing self-rule but also making Milan a great center of art, architecture, and learning. Having Leonardo da Vinci around for a number of years obviously helped. He rates his own museum in Milan.

One of our disappointments was finding the Ambrosian Library and Gallery closed for an extended period, *in restauro*. But that *is* one more reason for another visit, another voyage.

Slightly more than three weeks and something less than a month seems to be a sensible duration for such tours as ours. Anything shorter makes me feel that I haven't gotten my money's worth out of the air fare, while longer practically requires a power of attorney to get the utility bills paid at home, besides being potentially exhausting. The time comes to go home, reflect on it all, and dream of journeys yet to come. Six months of active touring might get you all around Italy. Better, we reasoned, to take it in smaller chunks and have another wonderful winter of anticipation, looking forward to still other magical cities and brushing up on our Italian to be ready for them.

The trip west back to the United States is more relaxed than the short night's sleeplessness of getting to Europe over the sea. Planes to New York leave at mid-day, and as the plane pursues the sun for a long day, you arrive in early afternoon with plenty of daylight to spare. We admired the handsome young airport terrorist protectors in their jungle fatigues with their Uzi machine guns. They were hospitable and smiling to the doting harmless, such as we seemed to be, except for one very pretty female lance corporal who clutched her gun with both hands and looked rapidly from left to right. Wisps of platinum blonde hair escaped from the sides of her camouflage covered helmet. I felt like reassuring her that there weren't any bombs in our bags, but decided she looked too intense to be teased.

As I peered down on the north Spanish coast an hour or so later and sampled the Pinot Grigio provided by Alitalia, I reflected on the advice given us by a lady of great travel experience we had asked for suggestions about which cities to visit in northern Italy.

"Will it be your first time in Italy?" she asked. I answered that it would indeed.

"Well, in that case," she said with a happy and expectant smile, "in that case you can't go wrong."

Finis

SOME SUGGESTIONS FOR FURTHER READING

While this is not a bibliography of all that we read about Italy, these titles are among the most interesting and the most useful books that we have seen. Some are old and a few are out of print but worth looking up in libraries or in secondhand bookstores.

Lives of the Most Excellent Painters, Sculptors and Architects, by Giorgio Vasari (Florence: 1550 and 1568) is a monumental work, which in some editions can run to as many as five volumes in Italian. There are, however, a number of good abridgments in English such as that published in paperback by Viking Penguin, New York and London, 1988. Although sometimes criticized as being of variable accuracy, the biographies of artists of the Renaissance are quite wonderfully fresh, even today. Vasari's personal relationship with Michelangelo makes that essay especially interesting.

A wonderfully detailed history is *Florence: The Biography of a City*, by Christopher Hibbert (New York: W. W. Norton, 1993). This book, as well as recounting the scandals and gory incidents that are missing from other histories, is beautifully illustrated.

Urbino: Historical Artistic Guide [English text], Italian text by Caimi Massimo (Gross, Rimini, n.d.), is a guide book available in Urbino. It gives an excellent portrait of this early Renaissance town and includes good color reproductions of Ucello's "Profanation of the Host."

Alternating between humorous and doomsday views of the Italian character, *The Italians: A Full-Length Portrait Featuring Their Manners and Morals*, by Luigi Barzini (New York: Macmillan, 1977), which was originally published in 1964, makes some predictions that have not as yet come about. It includes an interesting and somewhat sympathetic history of the Sicilian Mafia.

A Traveller in Italy, by H.V. Morton (New York: Dodd, Mead, 1964) rambles on about everything from the partisan execution of Mussolini to the frescoes of Florence and the poison antidotes of ancient Rome. Morton is a most genial traveling companion in northern Italy. For a happy blend of history, travellers tales, and sensitive description of the great works of art, Morton is the best. It is a pity that this book has been allowed to go out of print.

Cento Citta: A Guide to the "Hundred Cities & Towns" of Italy by Paul Hoffmann (New York: Henry Holt & Co., 1988) is necessarily brief (the author covers a hundred towns in a little more than 300 pages, and leaves out the larger cities), but he gives good material on small places that the standard guide books skip over.

As you might imagine from its source, *Let's Go Italy 1995,* by Let's Go Inc., a subsidiary of the Harvard University Student Agencies (New York: St. Martin's Press, 1995) this guide book is written for the young of heart, soul and body as well as for those of a limited purse. Travellers of a more sedate age may find some of its recommendations for lodging primitive, but choosing the most expensive listed will provide a perfectly decent place to stay. Recommendations of what to see and how to find it are breezy, incisive, irreverent and accurate.

We found the most useful of all guidebooks to be *Fielding's Italy 1993* by Lynn V. Foster (Redondo Beach, CA: Fielding Worldwide Inc., 1995). Hotels are well described and categorized as to cost with current update of the most recent season's prices (in Lira) in a special index by town in the back. These lists (with phone numbers in the next column) were the most often thumbed pages of any book we used. Although many expensive places are given, even the very cheapest in this book are clean, safe, and well run. We never went wrong bottom fishing from Fielding's list.

Italy: Michelin Tourist Guide, the "Green Guide," is published by Michelin Tyre, Ltd. It provides the essential tourist information on virtually every town of any size in Italy. Use the most recent edition you can find. This is a portable guidebook you can carry around with you. It also lists admission fees and hours of the museums and has an outline history of Italy in the first few pages. An essential *vade mecum*.

Long out of print, *The Life of Cesare Borgia, Duke of Valentinois and Romagna,* by Rafael Sabitini, is an entertaining biography that presents a persuasive defense of the life style of the Borgias, including Pope Alexander VI. Sabatini defends the honor of the often maligned Lucretia against the ungallant criticisms of Victor Hugo.

Isabella d'Este, Marchioness of Mantua 1474-1539: A Study of the Renaissance, by Julia Cartwright (Mrs. Ady), 2 vols., (London: John Murray, 1904). There are probably more recent editions of this great work, but finding the ancient original in a second-hand book store was a treat. The Victorian author skirts around some of the spicier incidents of the quattrocento but her indefatigable research into the lives of her subjects and liberal quotation from Isabella's letters (almost all of which still exist) make this one of the most authentically flavorful accounts of the period. Popes, poets, scholars, courtiers, warriors, painters, emperors and sculptors all knew and corresponded with "La prima donna del mundo." Almost all of the great characters of the Italian Renaissance are to be met with here.

Index